HAMMOND

Atlas of United States History

W9-CNU-715

Mapmakers for the 21st Century

Contents

Gazetteer of States, Territories and Possessions —— U-3
Native Americans —— U-4
Voyages of Discovery to America —— U-5
Voyages of Discovery to Asia and Africa —— U-5
Early Maps of the New World —— U-6
Exploration of the United States —— U-6
European Settlements on the North American Coast 1500–1600 —— U-7
European Powers in the New World —— U-7
Early Colonial Grants —— U-8–9
French and Indian Wars 1689–1763 —— U-10–11
France and Spain in Interior North America before 1763 —— U-11
Colonial America 1770 —— U-12–13
Colonial California 1769–1823 —— U-13
The American Revolution 1775–1781 —— U-14–15
Settlement of the United States 1770–1890 —— U-16
Expansion of the United States 1783–1898 —— U-16
Conflicting Claims to the West after the Treaty of 1783 —— U-17
The War of 1812 —— U-18–19
Naval Battles 1777–1815 —— U-19
Operations Against the Barbary States 1803–1815 —— U-19
Early Transportation 1783–1860 —— U-20
The Texas Revolution 1835–1836 —— U-21
The Mexican War 1846–1848 —— U-21
Free and Slave Areas 1821–1861 —— U-22–23
The Civil War 1861–1865 —— U-24–25
Slaves 1860; Cotton Production 1860 —— U-25
The Virginia Campaigns of the Civil War 1861–1865 —— U-26–27
The Battle of Gettysburg —— U-27
Reconstruction Period 1865–1877 —— U-28
Black Participation in Constitutional Conventions 1867–1868 —— U-28
Rich States and Poor States 1860 vs. 1880 —— U-29
The West 1860–1912 —— U-30–31
Indian Reservations and Army Posts in the West —— U-31
The Spanish-American War 1898 —— U-32
The United States in Middle America —— U-32–33
The United States in Latin America —— U-33
Growth of Industry and Cities —— U-34–35

Tariff Rates on Dutiable Imports —— U-36
Foreign Trade —— U-36
Exports; Imports —— U-37
Sources of Immigration —— U-38
Immigration Patterns of Major Foreign Groups 1821–1921 —— U-38
Total Immigration from all Countries —— U-38
Distribution of Foreign Born in United States 1910 —— U-39
World War I in Europe —— U-40
The Western Front —— U-40
The Western Front 1918, Reduction of the Salients and Final Offensive —— U-41
Europe in the 1920's —— U-41
The Great Depression —— U-42–43
Conservation of Natural Resources —— U-44–45
German Expansion 1935–1939 —— U-46
World War II 1939–1940 —— U-46
World War II, European Theater 1940–1945 —— U-47
Japanese Expansion 1875–1941 —— U-48
World War II, Pacific Theater 1941–1945 —— U-48–49
The World at War 1939–1945 —— U-49
United States in the Postwar World —— U-50–51
United States Interests in the Far East —— U-52
The Korean Conflict 1950–1953 —— U-53
The Vietnam Conflict 1961–1975 —— U-53
Ethnic Distribution; Immigration 1981–1990 —— U-54
Modern Urban Problems —— U-55
Growth of the United States Economy —— U-56–57
Alaska and Hawaii–Major Historical Events —— U-58
The Fifty States: Population Distribution, Rank by Area, Rank by Population, Years of Admission to the Union —— U-59
Population Characteristics —— U-60
Development of Political Parties, Party Strength in Presidential Elections —— U-61
Political Sectionalism, Presidential Electoral Vote by States and Parties —— U-62–65
Presidents of the United States —— U-65
Flags of American History —— U-66–67
United States Political Map —— U-68–69
Flags of States, Territories and Possessions —— U-70–71
Index —— U-72

REVISED 2001 EDITION

ENTIRE CONTENTS © COPYRIGHT MCMXCVII BY HAMMOND WORLD ATLAS CORPORATION

All rights reserved. No part of this book may be reproduced or utilized in any form or by any means, electronic or mechanical, including photocopying, recording or by any information storage and retrieval system, without permission in writing from the Publisher.

LIBRARY OF CONGRESS CATALOG CARD NUMBER 96-49621
ISBN 0-8437-1761-0 (sc)
ISBN 0-8437-1449-2 (hc)
PRINTED IN THE UNITED STATES OF AMERICA

Gazetteer of States, Territories and Possessions

State or Territory	Area (sq. mi.)†	Area (sq. km.)†	Population (2000)	Inhabitants per sq. mi. ††	Admitted to the Union	Settled at	Date
Alabama	52,237	135,293	4,447,100	87.6	Dec. 14, 1819	Mobile	1702
Alaska	615,230	1,593,444	626,932	1.1	Jan. 3, 1959	Sitka	1801
American Samoa	90	233	65,446§	849.9	*Feb. 16, 1900	....	....
Arizona	114,006	295,276	5,130,632	45.1	Feb. 14, 1912	Tucson	1752
Arkansas	53,182	137,742	2,673,400	51.3	Jun. 15, 1836	Arkansas Post	1685
California	158,869	411,470	33,871,648	217.2	Sept. 9, 1850	San Diego	1769
Colorado	104,100	269,618	4,301,261	41.5	Aug. 1, 1876	Near Denver	1858
Connecticut	5,544	14,358	3,405,565	702.9	Jan. 9, 1788	Windsor	1635
Delaware	2,396	6,206	783,600	400.8	Dec. 7, 1787	Cape Henlopen	1627
District of Columbia	68	177	572,059	9,378.0	** 1790-1791	....	1790
Florida	59,928	155,214	15,982,378	296.3	Mar. 3, 1845	St. Augustine	1565
Georgia	58,977	152,750	8,186,453	141.3	Jan. 2, 1788	Savannah	1733
Guam	217	561	154,623§	736.3	*Dec. 10, 1898	Agana	1668
Hawaii	6,459	16,729	1,211,537	188.6	Aug. 21, 1959	....	....
Idaho	83,574	216,456	1,293,953	15.6	July 3, 1890	Coeur d'Alene	1842
Illinois	57,918	150,007	12,419,293	223.4	Dec. 3, 1818	Kaskaskia	1720
Indiana	36,420	94,328	6,080,485	169.5	Dec. 11, 1816	Vincennes	1730
Iowa	56,276	145,754	2,926,324	52.4	Dec. 28, 1846	Burlington	1788
Kansas	82,282	213,110	2,688,418	32.9	Jan. 29, 1861	....	1831
Kentucky	40,411	104,665	4,041,769	101.7	June 1, 1792	Harrodsburg	1774
Louisiana	49,651	128,595	4,468,976	102.6	Apr. 30, 1812	Iberville	1699
Maine	33,741	87,388	1,274,923	41.3	Mar. 15, 1820	Bristol	1624
Maryland	12,297	31,849	5,296,486	541.8	Apr. 28, 1788	St. Mary's	1634
Massachusetts	9,241	23,934	6,349,097	810.0	Feb. 6, 1788	Plymouth	1620
Michigan	96,705	250,465	9,938,444	174.9	Jan. 26, 1837	Near Detroit	1650
Minnesota	86,943	225,182	4,919,479	61.8	May 11, 1858	St. Peter's River	1805
Mississippi	48,268	125,060	2,844,658	60.6	Dec. 10, 1817	Natchez	1716
Missouri	69,709	180,546	5,595,211	81.2	Aug. 10, 1821	St. Louis	1764
Montana	147,046	380,849	902,195	6.2	Nov. 8, 1889	....	1809
Nebraska	77,358	200,358	1,711,263	22.3	Mar. 1, 1867	Bellevue	1847
Nevada	110,567	286,367	1,998,257	18.2	Oct. 31, 1864	Genoa	1850
New Hampshire	9,283	24,044	1,235,786	137.8	June 21, 1788	Dover and Portsmouth	1623
New Jersey	8,215	21,277	8,414,350	1,134.2	Dec. 18, 1787	Bergen	1617
New Mexico	121,598	314,939	1,819,046	15.0	Jan. 6, 1912	Santa Fe	1605
New York	53,989	139,833	18,976,457	401.8	July 26, 1788	Manhattan Island	1614
North Carolina	52,672	136,421	8,049,313	165.2	Nov. 21, 1789	Albemarle	1650
North Dakota	70,704	183,123	642,200	9.3	Nov. 2, 1889	Pembina	1780
Northern Marianas	189	490	71,912§	401.7	Apr. 2, 1947	....	....
Ohio	44,828	116,103	11,353,140	277.2	Mar. 1, 1803	Marietta	1788
Oklahoma	69,903	181,048	3,450,654	50.2	Nov. 16, 1907	....	1889
Oregon	97,132	251,571	3,421,399	35.6	Feb. 14, 1859	Astoria	1810
Pennsylvania	46,058	119,291	12,281,054	274.0	Dec. 12, 1787	Delaware River	1682
Puerto Rico	3,508	9,085	3,808,610	1,111.4	*Dec. 10, 1898	Caparra	1510
Rhode Island	1,231	3,189	1,048,319	1,003.2	May 29, 1790	Providence	1636
South Carolina	31,189	80,779	4,012,012	133.2	May 23, 1788	Port Royal	1670
South Dakota	77,121	199,744	754,844	9.9	Nov. 2, 1889	Sioux Falls	1856
Tennessee	42,146	109,158	5,689,283	138.0	June 1, 1796	Ft. Loudon	1757
Texas	267,277	692,248	20,851,820	79.6	Dec. 29, 1845	Matagorda Bay	1686
Utah	84,904	219,902	2,233,169	27.2	Jan. 4, 1896	Salt Lake City	1847
Vermont	9,615	24,903	608,827	65.8	Mar. 4, 1791	Ft. Dummer	1764
Virginia	42,326	109,625	7,078,515	178.8	June 26, 1788	Jamestown	1607
Virgin Islands	171	443	120,917§	7,902.3	*Mar 31, 1917	St. Thomas I.	1657
Washington	70,637	182,949	5,894,121	88.5	Nov. 11, 1889	Astoria	1811
West Virginia	24,231	62,759	1,808,344	75.1	June 20, 1863	Wheeling	1774
Wisconsin	65,499	169,643	5,363,675	98.8	May 29, 1848	Green Bay	1670
Wyoming	97,818	253,349	493,782	5.1	July 10, 1890	Ft. Laramie	1834
United States	3,717,796	9,629,091	281,421,906	79.6	....	....	....
United States, Territories & Possessions	3,721,971	9,639,903	285,643,414	80.7	....	....	....

* Date of organization as Territory or acquisition by U.S.   ** Established under Acts of Congress   † Land and water.   †† Calculations based on land area.
§ Estimated population
Source: US Census Bureau

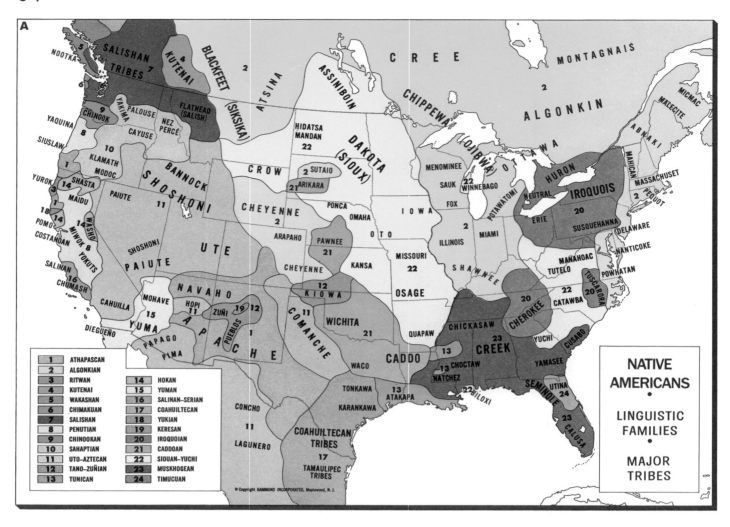

A

SALISHAN TRIBES 7
KUTENAI 4
NOOTKA 5
BLACKFEET (SIKSIKA)
2
ATSINA
ASSINIBOIN
CREE
MONTAGNAIS
CHIPPEWA (OJIBWA)
ALGONKIN
2
MICMAC
MALECITE
YAKIMA 9
PALOUSE
CHINOOK
FLATHEAD (SALISH)
YAQUINA
CAYUSE
NEZ PERCÉ
HIDATSA MANDAN 22
DAKOTA (SIOUX)
OTTAWA
MENOMINEE
HURON
IROQUOIS 20
ABNAKI
MASSACHUSET
SIUSLAW
8
KLAMATH
10
MODOC
BANNOCK
CROW
2 SUTAIO
ARIKARA 21
SAUK
WINNEBAGO 22
POTAWATOMI
NEUTRAL
ERIE
SUSQUEHANNA
PEQUOT
YUROK
SHASTA 14
SHOSHONI
CHEYENNE
PONCA
IOWA
FOX
2
MIAMI
ILLINOIS
DELAWARE
MAIDU
PAIUTE
2
MANAHOAC
NANTICOKE
POMO 18
WASHO 14
ARAPAHO
OMAHA
OTO
SHAWNEE
TUTELO
POWHATAN
TUSCARORA 22
COSTANOAN
MIWOK 8
UTE
PAWNEE 21
MISSOURI 22
KANSA
MANAHOAC 20
CATAWBA
SALINAN 16
YOKUTS
SHOSHONI
CHEYENNE
OSAGE
20 CHEROKEE
CHUMASH
PAIUTE
NAVAHO
KIOWA 12
WICHITA
CAHUILLA
MOHAVE
HOPI 11
ZUÑI 19 12
COMANCHE 11
QUAPAW
CHICKASAW 23
YUCHI
CUSABO
DIEGUEÑO
15
PUEBLOS
1
21
CREEK
YAMASEE
YUMA
PAPAGO
CADDO
13 CHOCTAW
13
NATCHEZ
SEMINOLE
UTINA 24
PIMA
WACO
TONKAWA
ATAKAPA 13
22 BILOXI
CONCHO
KARANKAWA
CALUSA 23
LAGUNERO
11
COAHUILTECAN TRIBES
17
TAMAULIPEC TRIBES

1	ATHAPASCAN	14	HOKAN
2	ALGONKIAN	15	YUMAN
3	RITWAN	16	SALINAN–SERIAN
4	KUTENAI	17	COAHUILTECAN
5	WAKASHAN	18	YUKIAN
6	CHIMAKUAN	19	KERESAN
7	SALISHAN	20	IROQUOIAN
8	PENUTIAN	21	CADDOAN
9	CHINOOKAN	22	SIOUAN–YUCHI
10	SAHAPTIAN	23	MUSKHOGEAN
11	UTO–AZTECAN	24	TIMUCUAN
12	TANO–ZUÑIAN		
13	TUNICAN		

© Copyright HAMMOND INCORPORATED, Maplewood, N.J.

NATIVE AMERICANS

•

LINGUISTIC FAMILIES

•

MAJOR TRIBES

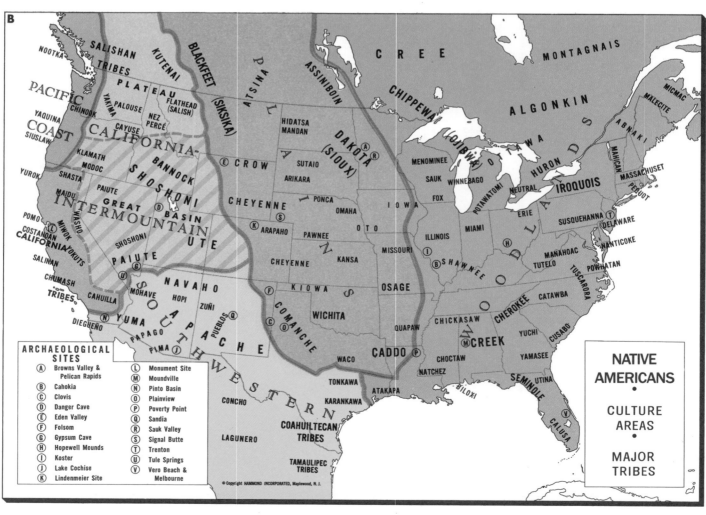

B

PACIFIC
NOOTKA
SALISHAN TRIBES
KUTENAI
PLATEAU
BLACKFEET (SIKSIKA)
ATSINA
ASSINIBOIN
CREE
MONTAGNAIS
CHINOOK
YAKIMA
PALOUSE
FLATHEAD (SALISH)
CAYUSE
NEZ PERCÉ
CHIPPEWA (OJIBWA)
ALGONKIN
MICMAC
MALECITE
COAST
YAQUINA
CALIFORNIA-
HIDATSA MANDAN
DAKOTA (SIOUX)
CROW Ⓔ
SUTAIO
ARIKARA Ⓡ
OTTAWA
MENOMINEE
HURON
IROQUOIS
ABNAKI
MASSACHUSET
SIUSLAW
YUROK
KLAMATH
MODOC
BANNOCK
SHOSHONI
GREAT BASIN Ⓓ
CHEYENNE
PONCA
SAUK
WINNEBAGO
POTAWATOMI
NEUTRAL
ERIE
SUSQUEHANNA
PEQUOT
SHASTA
MAIDU
PAIUTE
Ⓚ ARAPAHO Ⓢ
PAWNEE
IOWA
FOX
MIAMI
ILLINOIS
DELAWARE
Ⓣ
POMO
WASHO
INTERMOUNTAIN
UTE
MISSOURI Ⓘ
Ⓗ
TUTELO
POWHATAN
NANTICOKE
COSTANOAN Ⓛ
MIWOK
CALIFORNIA
SHOSHONI
CHEYENNE
KANSA
Ⓑ SHAWNEE
MANAHOAC
TUSCARORA
SALINAN
YOKUTS
PAIUTE Ⓖ
OSAGE
CATAWBA
CHUMASH
Ⓤ
NAVAHO
KIOWA Ⓕ
WICHITA
CHICKASAW
CHEROKEE
TRIBES
MOHAVE
HOPI
ZUÑI
Ⓠ
QUAPAW
YUCHI
CUSABO
CAHUILLA
SOUTH
COMANCHE Ⓒ
Ⓜ CREEK
YAMASEE
DIEGUEÑO Ⓝ
YUMA
PUEBLOS
CADDO Ⓟ
CHOCTAW
NATCHEZ
SEMINOLE
UTINA
PAPAGO
APACHE
WACO
PIMA Ⓙ
TONKAWA
SOUTHWESTERN
KARANKAWA
ATAKAPA
BILOXI
CONCHO
CALUSA Ⓥ
LAGUNERO
COAHUILTECAN TRIBES
TAMAULIPEC TRIBES

© Copyright HAMMOND INCORPORATED, Maplewood, N.J.

ARCHAEOLOGICAL SITES

Ⓐ	Browns Valley & Pelican Rapids	Ⓛ	Monument Site
Ⓑ	Cahokia	Ⓜ	Moundville
Ⓒ	Clovis	Ⓝ	Pinto Basin
Ⓓ	Danger Cave	Ⓞ	Plainview
Ⓔ	Eden Valley	Ⓟ	Poverty Point
Ⓕ	Folsom	Ⓠ	Sandia
Ⓖ	Gypsum Cave	Ⓡ	Sauk Valley
Ⓗ	Hopewell Mounds	Ⓢ	Signal Butte
Ⓘ	Koster	Ⓣ	Trenton
Ⓙ	Lake Cochise	Ⓤ	Tule Springs
Ⓚ	Lindenmeier Site	Ⓥ	Vero Beach & Melbourne

NATIVE AMERICANS

•

CULTURE AREAS

•

MAJOR TRIBES

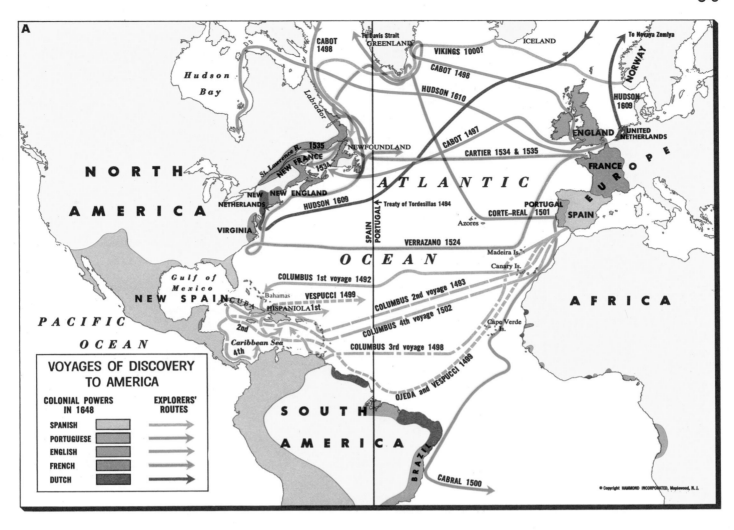

A

VOYAGES OF DISCOVERY
TO AMERICA

COLONIAL POWERS
IN 1648

EXPLORERS'
ROUTES

SPANISH

PORTUGUESE

ENGLISH

FRENCH

DUTCH

© Copyright HAMMOND INCORPORATED, Maplewood, N.J.

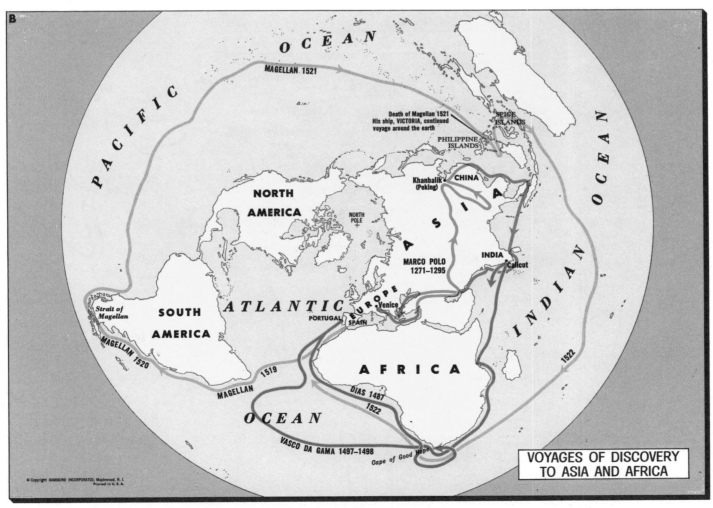

B

VOYAGES OF DISCOVERY
TO ASIA AND AFRICA

© Copyright HAMMOND INCORPORATED, Maplewood, N.J.
Printed in U.S.A.

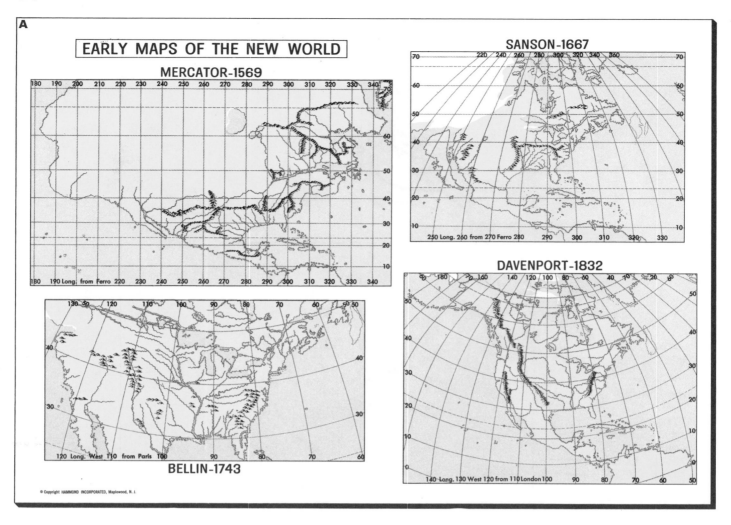

A

EARLY MAPS OF THE NEW WORLD

MERCATOR-1569

SANSON-1667

DAVENPORT-1832

BELLIN-1743

© Copyright HAMMOND INCORPORATED, Maplewood, N. J.

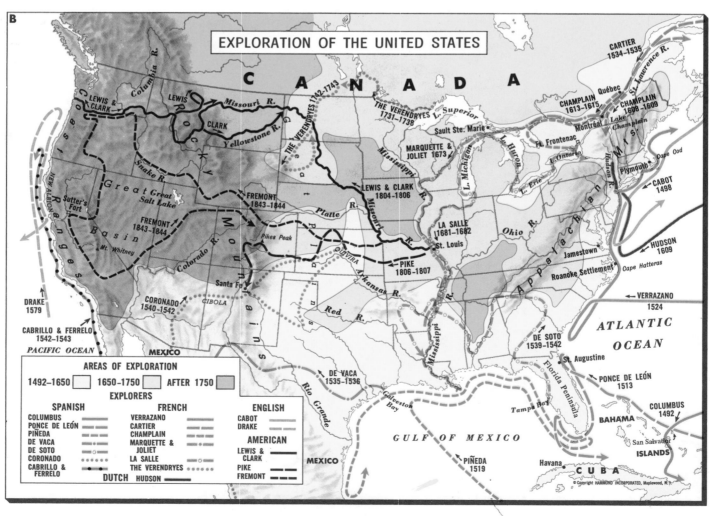

B

EXPLORATION OF THE UNITED STATES

AREAS OF EXPLORATION

1492–1650 1650–1750 AFTER 1750

EXPLORERS

SPANISH
COLUMBUS
PONCE DE LEÓN
PIÑEDA
DE VACA
DE SOTO
CORONADO
CABRILLO & FERRELO

FRENCH
VERRAZANO
CARTIER
CHAMPLAIN
MARQUETTE & JOLIET
LA SALLE
THE VERENDRYES

DUTCH HUDSON

ENGLISH
CABOT
DRAKE

AMERICAN
LEWIS & CLARK
PIKE
FREMONT

© Copyright HAMMOND INCORPORATED, Maplewood, N. J.

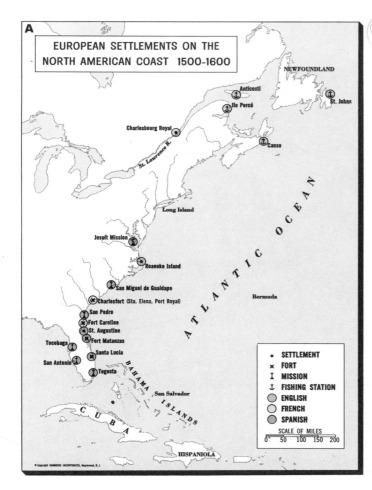

A

EUROPEAN SETTLEMENTS ON THE NORTH AMERICAN COAST 1500-1600

NEWFOUNDLAND

Anticosti
Ile Percé
St. Johns
Charlesbourg Royal
Canso
St. Lawrence R.

Long Island

Jesuit Mission
Roanoke Island

San Miguel de Gualdape
Charlesfort (Sta. Elena, Port Royal)
San Pedro
Fort Caroline
St. Augustine
Tocobaga
Fort Matanzas
Santa Lucia
San Antonio
Tegesta

BAHAMA ISLANDS

San Salvador

CUBA

ATLANTIC OCEAN

Bermuda

HISPANIOLA

- SETTLEMENT
× FORT
↨ MISSION
↧ FISHING STATION
⬤ ENGLISH
◯ FRENCH
⬤ SPANISH

SCALE OF MILES
0 50 100 150 200

© Copyright HAMMOND INCORPORATED, Maplewood, N.J.

B

EUROPEAN POWERS IN THE NEW WORLD 1682

HUDSON BAY

HUDSON'S BAY COMPANY

NEWFOUND-LAND

Great Lakes

NEW FRANCE

ACADIA

St. Lawrence R.

NEW ENGLAND

LOUISIANA

Mississippi R.

ENGLISH COLONIES

VIRGINIA

CAROLINA

FLORIDA

PACIFIC OCEAN

GULF OF MEXICO

CUBA

NEW SPAIN

CARIBBEAN SEA

ATLANTIC OCEAN

NEW GRANADA

ENGLISH
FRENCH
SPANISH

SCALE OF MILES
0 200 400 600

© Copyright HAMMOND INCORPORATED, Maplewood, N.J.

C

EUROPEAN POWERS IN THE NEW WORLD 1713

HUDSON BAY

HUDSON'S BAY COMPANY

NEWFOUND-LAND

Great Lakes

NEW FRANCE

ISLE ROYALE

St. Lawrence R.

NOVA SCOTIA

NEW ENGLAND

LOUISIANA

Mississippi R.

ENGLISH COLONIES

VIRGINIA

CAROLINA

TEXAS

FLORIDA

PACIFIC OCEAN

GULF OF MEXICO

CUBA

ST. DOMINGUE (HAITI)

NEW SPAIN

CARIBBEAN SEA

ATLANTIC OCEAN

NEW GRANADA

ENGLISH
FRENCH
SPANISH

SCALE OF MILES
0 200 400 600

© Copyright HAMMOND INCORPORATED, Maplewood, N.J.

D

EUROPEAN POWERS IN THE NEW WORLD 1763

RUSSIANS

HUDSON BAY

HUDSON'S BAY COMPANY

NEWFOUND-LAND

Great Lakes

QUEBEC

St. Lawrence R.

NOVA SCOTIA

NEW ENGLAND

LOUISIANA

Mississippi R.

ENGLISH COLONIES

VIRGINIA

CAROLINAS

TEXAS

FLORIDA

PACIFIC OCEAN

GULF OF MEXICO

CUBA

ST. DOMINGUE (HAITI)

NEW SPAIN

CARIBBEAN SEA

ATLANTIC OCEAN

NEW GRANADA

ENGLISH
FRENCH
SPANISH

SCALE OF MILES
0 200 400 600

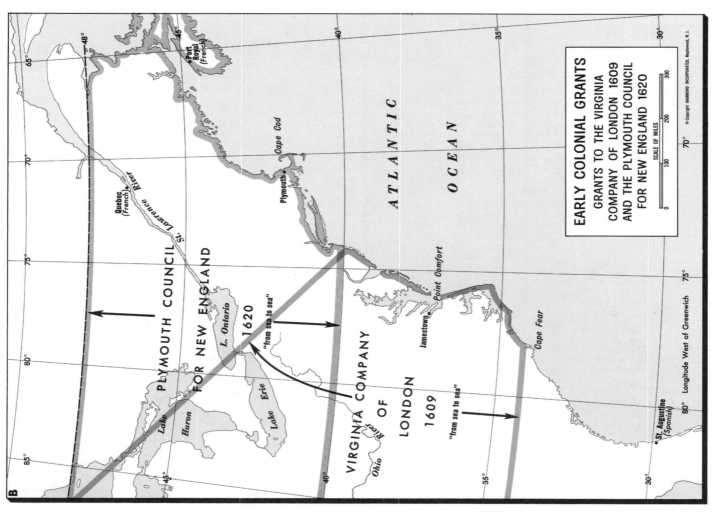

EARLY COLONIAL GRANTS
GRANTS TO THE VIRGINIA
COMPANY OF LONDON 1609
AND THE PLYMOUTH COUNCIL
FOR NEW ENGLAND 1620

SCALE OF MILES

© Copyright HAMMOND INCORPORATED, Maplewood, N.J.

Labels on map B:

Port Royal (French)

Quebec (French)

St. Lawrence River

Lake Huron

Lake Erie

L. Ontario

Ohio River

Plymouth • Cape Cod

PLYMOUTH COUNCIL FOR NEW ENGLAND 1620

"from sea to sea"

VIRGINIA COMPANY OF LONDON 1609

"from sea to sea"

Jamestown • Point Comfort

Cape Fear

St. Augustine (Spanish)

ATLANTIC OCEAN

Longitude West of Greenwich

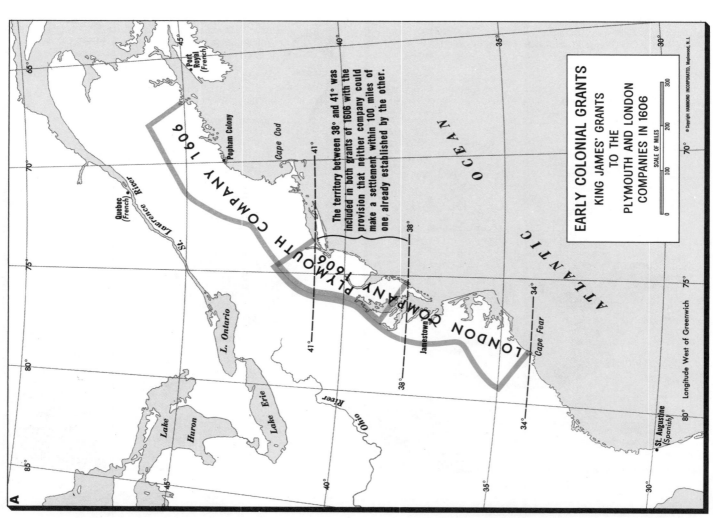

EARLY COLONIAL GRANTS
KING JAMES' GRANTS
TO THE
PLYMOUTH AND LONDON
COMPANIES IN 1606

SCALE OF MILES

© Copyright HAMMOND INCORPORATED, Maplewood, N.J.

Labels on map A:

Port Royal (French)

Quebec (French)

St. Lawrence River

Lake Huron

Lake Erie

L. Ontario

Ohio River

Popham Colony

Cape Cod

PLYMOUTH COMPANY 1606

The territory between 38° and 41° was included in both grants of 1606 with the provision that neither company could make a settlement within 100 miles of one already established by the other.

LONDON COMPANY 1606

Jamestown • Point Comfort

Cape Fear

St. Augustine (Spanish)

ATLANTIC OCEAN

Longitude West of Greenwich

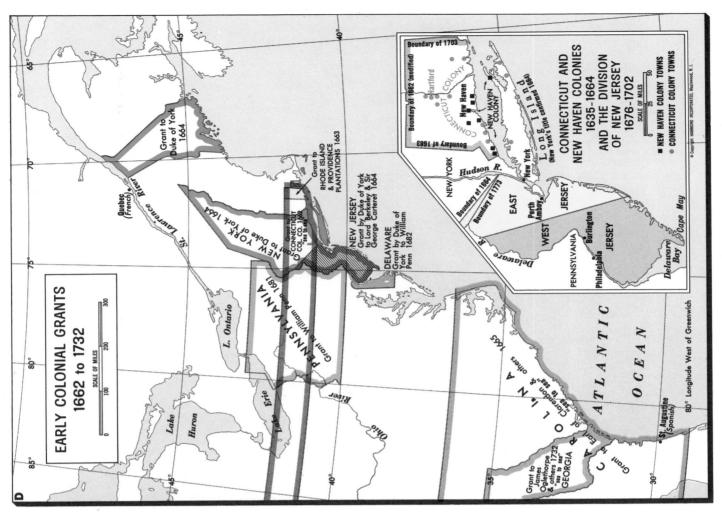

EARLY COLONIAL GRANTS 1662 to 1732

SCALE OF MILES
0   100   200   300

Quebec (French)
St. Lawrence River
L. Ontario
Lake Erie
Lake Huron
Ohio River

Grant to Duke of York 1664

PENNSYLVANIA
Grant to William Penn 1681

NEW YORK
Grant to Duke of York 1664

CONNECTICUT COL. CO. 1662 "sea to sea"

Grant to RHODE ISLAND & PROVIDENCE PLANTATIONS 1663

NEW JERSEY
Grant by Duke of York to Lord Berkeley & Sir George Carteret 1664

DELAWARE
Grant by Duke of York to William Penn 1682

CAROLINA
Clarendon & others 1665

Fort ...

GEORGIA
Grant to James Oglethorpe & others 1732 "sea to sea"

St. Augustine (Spanish)

80° Longitude West of Greenwich

ATLANTIC OCEAN

CONNECTICUT AND NEW HAVEN COLONIES 1635-1664 AND THE DIVISION OF NEW JERSEY 1676-1702

SCALE OF MILES
0   50

Boundary of 1703
Boundary of 1662 (modified)
Boundary of 1683
Boundary of 1664 (New York's title confirmed 1650)

Hartford
CONNECTICUT COLONY
New Haven
NEW HAVEN COLONY
Long Island (1650)

NEW YORK
New York
Hudson R.
Boundary of 1664
Boundary of 1773

EAST JERSEY
Perth Amboy

WEST JERSEY
Burlington

PENNSYLVANIA
Philadelphia

Delaware Bay
Cape May

- NEW HAVEN COLONY TOWNS
- CONNECTICUT COLONY TOWNS

© Copyright HAMMOND INCORPORATED, Maplewood, N.J.

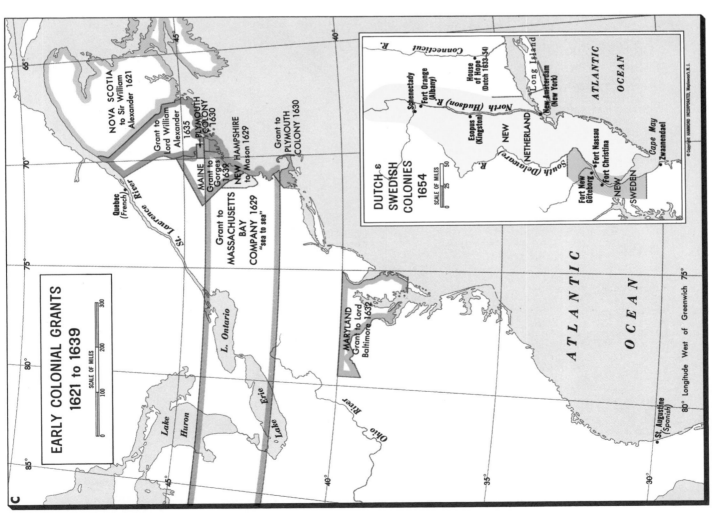

EARLY COLONIAL GRANTS 1621 to 1639

SCALE OF MILES
0   100   200   300

Quebec (French)
St. Lawrence River
L. Ontario
Lake Erie
Lake Huron
Ohio River

NOVA SCOTIA to Sir William Alexander 1621

Grant to Lord William Alexander 1635

PLYMOUTH COLONY 1630

MAINE
Grant to Gorges 1639

NEW HAMPSHIRE
to Mason 1629

Grant to MASSACHUSETTS BAY COMPANY 1629 "sea to sea"

Grant to PLYMOUTH COLONY 1630

MARYLAND
Grant to Lord Baltimore 1632

St. Augustine (Spanish)

80° Longitude West of Greenwich   75°

ATLANTIC OCEAN

DUTCH & SWEDISH COLONIES 1654

SCALE OF MILES
0   25   50

Schenectady
Fort Orange (Albany)
House of Hope (Dutch 1633-54)
Connecticut R.
Long Island
North (Hudson) R.
Esopus (Kingston)
NEW NETHERLAND
New Amsterdam (New York)
ATLANTIC OCEAN

South (Delaware) R.
Fort Nassau
Fort Christina
NEW SWEDEN
Fort New Göteborg
Zwaanendael
Cape May

© Copyright HAMMOND INCORPORATED, Maplewood, N.J.

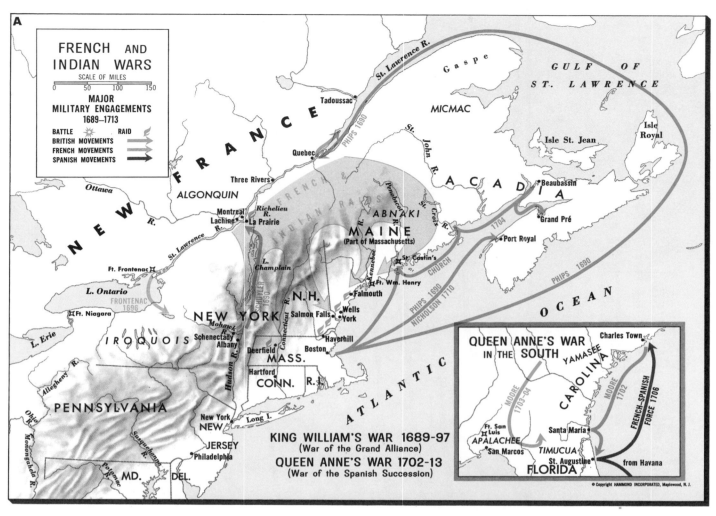

A

FRENCH AND INDIAN WARS
SCALE OF MILES
0   50   100   150

MAJOR
MILITARY ENGAGEMENTS
1689–1713

BATTLE ✴   RAID 🏹
BRITISH MOVEMENTS ⟶
FRENCH MOVEMENTS ⟹
SPANISH MOVEMENTS ⟹

GULF OF ST. LAWRENCE

St. Lawrence R.

Gaspe

MICMAC

Isle Royal

Isle St. Jean

NEW FRANCE

Tadoussac

Quebec

Three Rivers

ALGONQUIN

Ottawa

Montreal
Lachine   La Prairie

Richelieu R.

St. Lawrence

Ft. Frontenac

L. Ontario

FRONTENAC 1696

Ft. Niagara

L. Erie

IROQUOIS

Allegheny R.

Ohio R.

Monongahela R.

PENNSYLVANIA

Susquehanna R.

Potomac R.

MD.   DEL.

Philadelphia

NEW JERSEY

New York   Long I.

NEW

CONN.

Hartford

R.I.

MASS.

Boston

Deerfield

Schenectady
Albany

Mohawk R.

Hudson R.

NEW YORK

L. Champlain

N.H.

Connecticut R.

Salmon Falls

Wells
York

Haverhill

Falmouth

Ft. Wm. Henry

St. Castin's

Kennebec R.

MAINE
(Part of Massachusetts)

ABNAKI

Penobscot R.

St. Croix R.

St. John R.

ACADIA

Beaubassin

Grand Pré

Port Royal

1704

CHURCH

PHIPS 1690

NICHOLSON 1710

PHIPS 1690

ATLANTIC OCEAN

FRENCH INDIAN RAIDS

SCHUYLER 1690

KING WILLIAM'S WAR 1689-97
(War of the Grand Alliance)
QUEEN ANNE'S WAR 1702-13
(War of the Spanish Succession)

QUEEN ANNE'S WAR IN THE SOUTH

Charles Town

CAROLINA

YAMASEE

MOORE 1703-04

MOORE 1702

FRENCH-SPANISH FORCE 1706

Ft. San Luis

APALACHEE

San Marcos

Santa Maria

TIMUCUA

St. Augustine

FLORIDA

from Havana

© Copyright HAMMOND INCORPORATED, Maplewood, N.J.

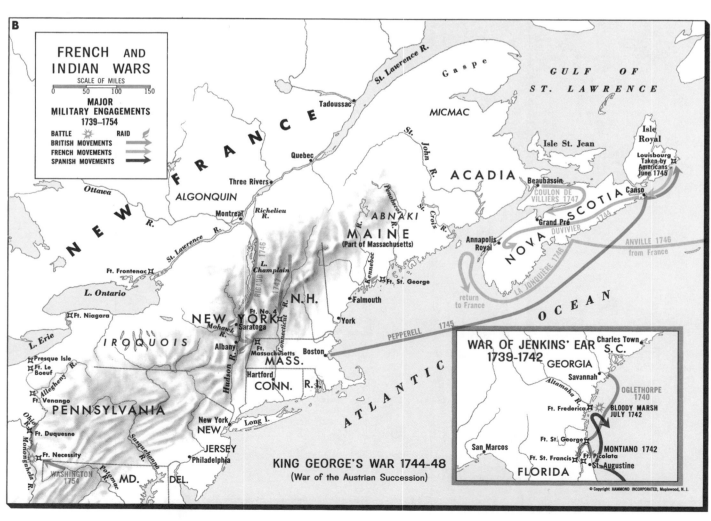

B

FRENCH AND INDIAN WARS
SCALE OF MILES
0   50   100   150

MAJOR
MILITARY ENGAGEMENTS
1739–1754

BATTLE ✴   RAID 🏹
BRITISH MOVEMENTS ⟶
FRENCH MOVEMENTS ⟹
SPANISH MOVEMENTS ⟹

GULF OF ST. LAWRENCE

St. Lawrence R.

Gaspe

MICMAC

Isle Royal

Louisbourg Taken by Americans June 1745

Isle St. Jean

NEW FRANCE

Tadoussac

Quebec

Three Rivers

ALGONQUIN

Ottawa

Montreal

Richelieu R.

St. Lawrence R.

Ft. Frontenac

L. Ontario

Ft. Niagara

L. Erie

IROQUOIS

Presque Isle
Ft. Le Boeuf

Ft. Allegheny

Ft. Venango

Allegheny R.

Ohio R.

Ft. Duquesne

Ft. Necessity

Monongahela R.

WASHINGTON 1754

PENNSYLVANIA

Susquehanna R.

Potomac R.

MD.   DEL.

Philadelphia

NEW JERSEY

New York   Long I.

NEW

CONN.

Hartford

R.I.

MASS.

Boston

Albany

Ft. Massachusetts

Saratoga

Ft. No. 4

Mohawk R.

Hudson R.

NEW YORK

RIGAUD 1746

L. Champlain

N.H.

Connecticut R.

York

Falmouth

Ft. St. George

Kennebec R.

MAINE
(Part of Massachusetts)

ABNAKI

Penobscot R.

St. Croix R.

St. John R.

ACADIA

Beaubassin

Grand Pré

Annapolis Royal

NOVA SCOTIA

Canso

DUVIVIER 1744

COULON DE VILLIERS 1747

LA JONQUIÈRE 1746

ANVILLE 1746 from France

return to France

PEPPERELL 1745

ATLANTIC OCEAN

KING GEORGE'S WAR 1744-48
(War of the Austrian Succession)

WAR OF JENKINS' EAR 1739-1742

Charles Town
S.C.

GEORGIA

Savannah

Altamaha R.

Ft. Frederica

OGLETHORPE 1740

BLOODY MARSH JULY 1742

San Marcos

Ft. St. George

Ft. St. Francis

Ft. Picolata

St. Augustine

MONTIANO 1742

FLORIDA

© Copyright HAMMOND INCORPORATED, Maplewood, N.J.

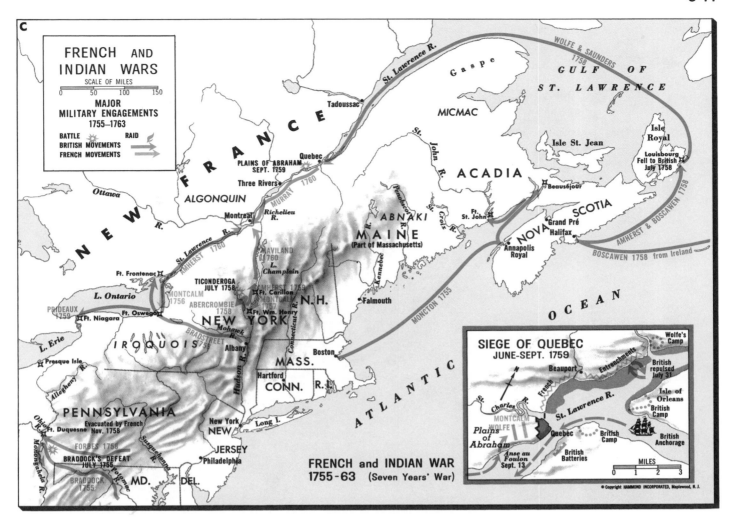

C

FRENCH AND INDIAN WARS

SCALE OF MILES
0   50   100   150

MAJOR MILITARY ENGAGEMENTS 1755–1763

BATTLE ✦   RAID →
BRITISH MOVEMENTS →
FRENCH MOVEMENTS →

NEW FRANCE

GULF OF ST. LAWRENCE

WOLFE & SAUNDERS 1758

St. Lawrence R.   Gaspe

Tadoussac

MICMAC

Isle St. Jean

Isle Royal

Louisbourg Fell to British July 1758

AMHERST & BOSCAWEN 1758

St. John R.

ACADIA

Quebec

PLAINS OF ABRAHAM SEPT. 1759

Three Rivers

ALGONQUIN

MURRAY 1760

Montreal   Richelieu R.

Beauséjour

Ft. St. John

BOSCAWEN 1758 from Ireland

Ottawa

St. Lawrence R.

AMHERST 1760

Ft. Frontenac

St. Croix

ABNAKI

MAINE (Part of Massachusetts)

Penobscot R.

Kennebec

NOVA SCOTIA

Grand Pré

Halifax

Annapolis Royal

Moncton 1755

HAVILAND 1760

L. Champlain

AMHERST 1759

MONTCALM 1756

TICONDEROGA JULY 1758

ABERCROMBIE 1758

Ft. Carillon

MONTCALM

Ft. Wm. Henry

N.H.

Falmouth

PRIDEAUX 1759

Ft. Niagara

Ft. Oswego

NEW YORK

BRADSTREET 1758

Mohawk R.

Albany

Boston

L. Ontario

L. Erie

Presque Isle

IROQUOIS

Hudson R.

MASS.

Hartford   CONN.   R.I.

Allegheny R.

PENNSYLVANIA

Ohio R.

Ft. Duquesne Evacuated by French Nov. 1758

FORBES 1758

New York

Long I.

NEW JERSEY

ATLANTIC

OCEAN

Monongahela R.

BRADDOCK'S DEFEAT JULY 1755

BRADDOCK 1755

Susquehanna R.

Potomac R.

Philadelphia

MD.   DEL.

FRENCH and INDIAN WAR 1755-63 (Seven Years' War)

SIEGE OF QUEBEC JUNE–SEPT. 1759

Beauport   Entrenchments

British repulsed July 31

St. Charles R.

MONTCALM

French

St. Lawrence R.

Isle of Orleans

British Camp

WOLFE

Plains of Abraham

Quebec

British Camp

Anse au Foulon Sept. 13

British Batteries

British Anchorage

MILES
0   1   2   3

© Copyright HAMMOND INCORPORATED, Maplewood, N.J.

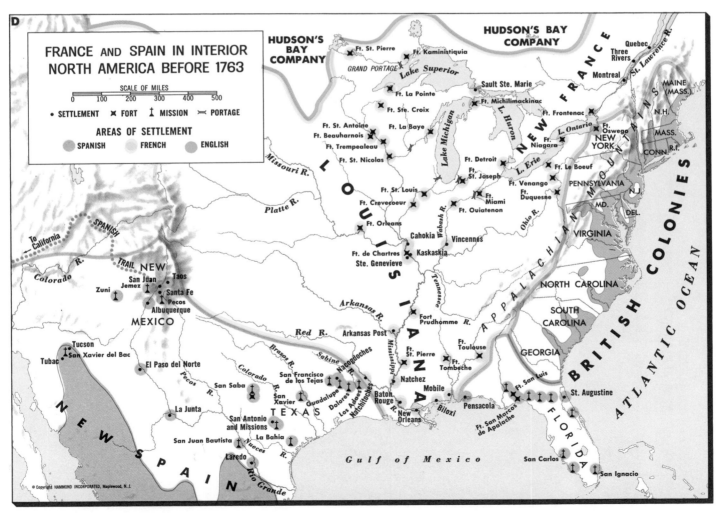

D

FRANCE AND SPAIN IN INTERIOR NORTH AMERICA BEFORE 1763

SCALE OF MILES
0   100   200   300   400   500

● SETTLEMENT   ✕ FORT   ⚵ MISSION   ⊱ PORTAGE

AREAS OF SETTLEMENT
SPANISH   FRENCH   ENGLISH

HUDSON'S BAY COMPANY

HUDSON'S BAY COMPANY

Ft. St. Pierre   Ft. Kaministiquia

GRAND PORTAGE   Lake Superior

Sault Ste. Marie

Ft. La Pointe

Ft. Ste. Croix

Ft. Michilimackinac

Quebec   Three Rivers

NEW FRANCE

Montreal   St. Lawrence R.

MAINE (MASS.)

N.H.

Ft. Frontenac

L. Ontario   Ft. Oswego

MASS.

CONN.   R.I.

Ft. St. Antoine

Ft. Beauharnois

Ft. Trempealeau

Ft. La Baye

L. Huron

Lake Michigan

Ft. Detroit

Ft. Niagara

L. Erie

Ft. Le Boeuf

NEW YORK

Ft. St. Nicolas

Missouri R.

Ft. St. Louis

Ft. St. Joseph

Ft. Venango

PENNSYLVANIA

Platte R.

Ft. Crevecoeur

Ft. Miami

Ft. Duquesne

MD.   N.J.   DEL.

Ft. Orleans

Ft. Ouiatenon

Wabash R.

Ohio R.

APPALACHIAN MOUNTAINS

VIRGINIA

L O U I S I A N A

Cahokia

Vincennes

To California

SPANISH TRAIL

Colorado R.

Ft. de Chartres

Kaskaskia

Ste. Genevieve

NEW MEXICO

Taos

San Juan

Jemez

Santa Fe

Pecos

Albuquerque

Arkansas R.

Tennessee R.

NORTH CAROLINA

BRITISH COLONIES

Zuni

MEXICO

Red R.

Arkansas Post

Fort Prudhomme

Ft. Toulouse

SOUTH CAROLINA

Tucson

San Xavier del Bac

Tubac

El Paso del Norte

Pecos R.

Brazos R.

Colorado R.

San Saba

San Francisco de los Tejas

Sabine R.

Natchitoches

Ft. St. Pierre

Ft. Tombeche

GEORGIA

ATLANTIC OCEAN

San Xavier

Guadalupe

Dolores

Los Adaes

Natchitoches

Natchez

Baton Rouge

Mobile

Pensacola

Ft. San Luis

St. Augustine

San Antonio and Missions

TEXAS

New Orleans

Biloxi

Ft. San Marcos de Apalache

FLORIDA

La Bahia

San Juan Bautista

Nueces R.

Laredo

Rio Grande

NEW SPAIN

Gulf of Mexico

San Carlos

San Ignacio

© Copyright HAMMOND INCORPORATED, Maplewood, N.J.

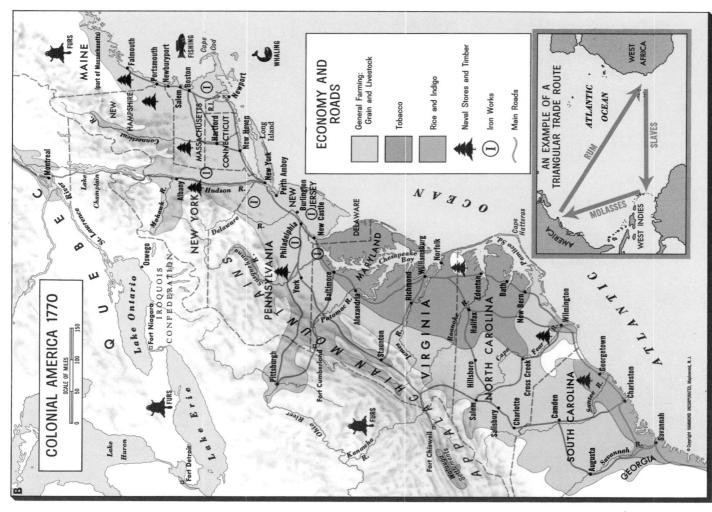

COLONIAL AMERICA 1770 (B)

ECONOMY AND ROADS

- General Farming: Grain and Livestock
- Tobacco
- Rice and Indigo
- 🌲 Naval Stores and Timber
- Ⓘ Iron Works
- ⌇ Main Roads

AN EXAMPLE OF A TRIANGULAR TRADE ROUTE

WEST AFRICA — SLAVES — WEST INDIES — MOLASSES — AMERICA — RUM — ATLANTIC OCEAN

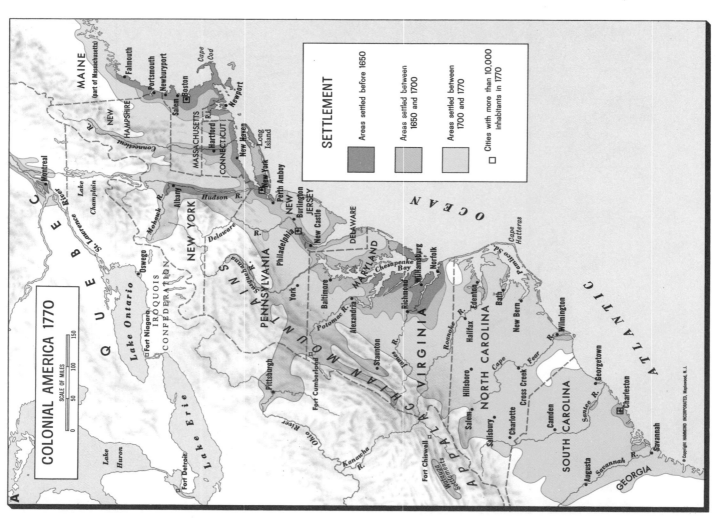

COLONIAL AMERICA 1770 (A)

SETTLEMENT

- Areas settled before 1650
- Areas settled between 1650 and 1700
- Areas settled between 1700 and 1770
- ☐ Cities with more than 10,000 inhabitants in 1770

© Copyright HAMMOND INCORPORATED, Maplewood, N.J.

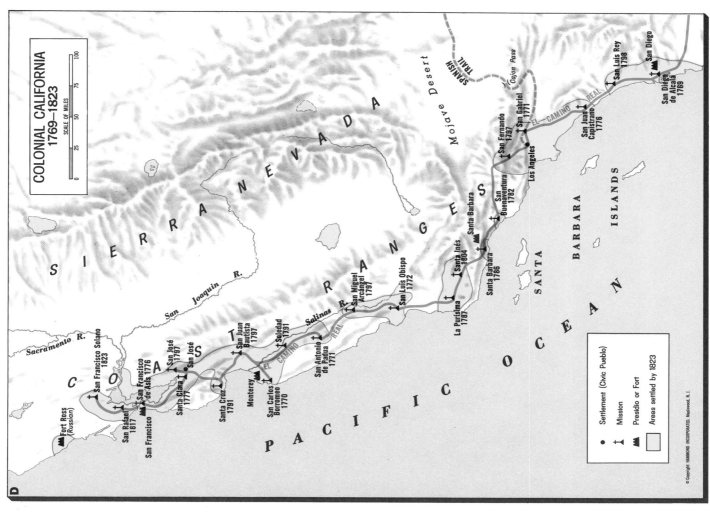

COLONIAL CALIFORNIA 1769–1823

SCALE OF MILES
0 25 50 75 100

SIERRA NEVADA

COAST RANGES

Sacramento R.

San Joaquin R.

Salinas R.

Mojave Desert

SPANISH TRAIL

Cajon Pass

Settlement (Civic Pueblo)
Mission
Presidio or Fort
Areas settled by 1823

Fort Ross (Russian)
San Rafael 1817
San Francisco Solano 1823
San Francisco de Asis 1776
San Francisco
Santa Clara 1777
San José 1797
San José
Santa Cruz 1791
San Juan Bautista 1797
Monterey
San Carlos Borromeo 1770
San Antonio de Padua 1771
Soledad 1791
San Miguel Arcángel 1797
San Luis Obispo 1772
La Purísima 1787
Santa Inés 1804
Santa Barbara 1786
Santa Barbara
San Buenaventura 1782
San Fernando 1797
San Gabriel 1771
Los Angeles
San Juan Capistrano 1776
San Luis Rey 1798
San Diego
San Diego de Alcalá 1769

EL CAMINO REAL

SANTA BARBARA ISLANDS

PACIFIC OCEAN

© Copyright HAMMOND INCORPORATED, Maplewood, N.J.

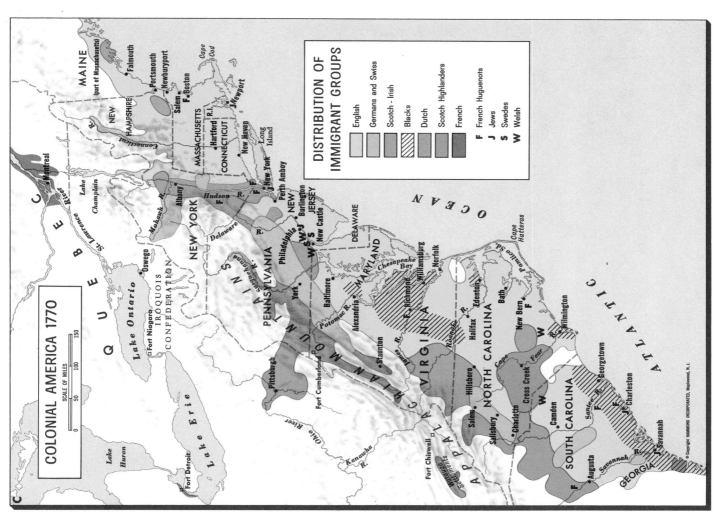

COLONIAL AMERICA 1770

SCALE OF MILES
0 50 100 150

DISTRIBUTION OF IMMIGRANT GROUPS

English
Germans and Swiss
Scotch-Irish
Blacks
Dutch
Scotch Highlanders
French
F French Huguenots
J Jews
S Swedes
W Welsh

QUEBEC

Lake Huron
Lake Erie
Lake Ontario
St. Lawrence River
Lake Champlain

Montreal
Oswego
Fort Niagara
Fort Detroit

IROQUOIS CONFEDERATION

Ohio River
Kanawha R.

Fort Pitt (Pittsburgh)
Fort Cumberland
Fort Chiswell

APPALACHIAN UNKNOWN

MAINE (part of Massachusetts)
Falmouth
Portsmouth
Newburyport
NEW HAMPSHIRE
Salem
F-Boston
Cape Cod
MASSACHUSETTS
Hartford
R.I.
CONNECTICUT
Newport
New Haven
Long Island
New York
Perth Amboy
Albany
Mohawk R.
Hudson R.
Connecticut R.
NEW YORK
NEW JERSEY
Burlington
Delaware R.
Philadelphia
New Castle
DELAWARE
PENNSYLVANIA
Susquehanna R.
York
Baltimore
MARYLAND
Chesapeake Bay
Potomac R.
Alexandria
Staunton
VIRGINIA
Richmond
Williamsburg
Norfolk
Roanoke R.
Edenton
Bath
Halifax
Hillsboro
NORTH CAROLINA
Salisbury
Salem
Charlotte
Cross Creek
New Bern
Cape Fear
Wilmington
Camden
SOUTH CAROLINA
Georgetown
Charleston
Augusta
Savannah R.
Santee R.
GEORGIA
Savannah

ATLANTIC OCEAN

Cape Hatteras
Pamlico Sd.

© Copyright HAMMOND INCORPORATED, Maplewood, N.J.

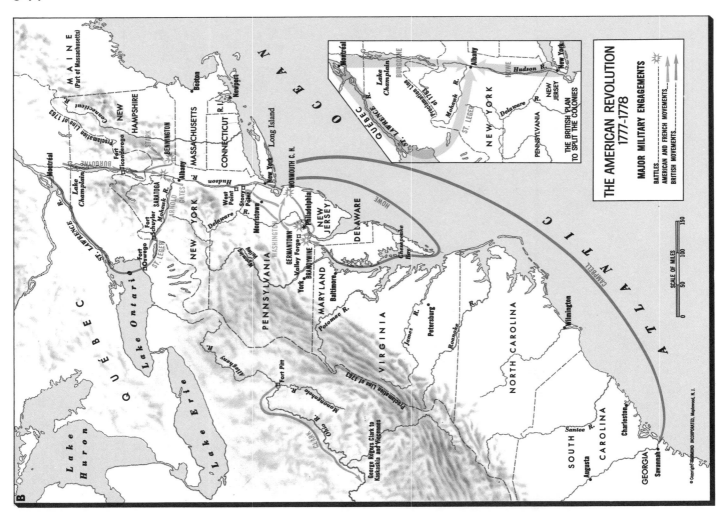

THE AMERICAN REVOLUTION
1777-1778

MAJOR MILITARY ENGAGEMENTS

BATTLES.
AMERICAN AND FRENCH MOVEMENTS.
BRITISH MOVEMENTS.

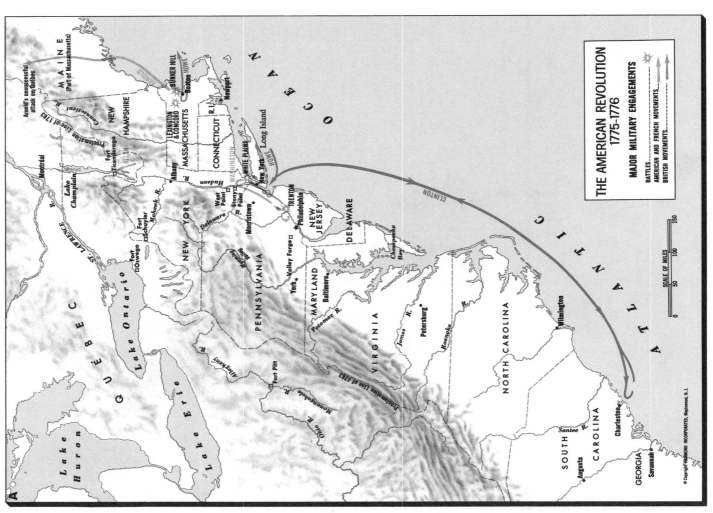

THE AMERICAN REVOLUTION
1775-1776

MAJOR MILITARY ENGAGEMENTS

BATTLES.
AMERICAN AND FRENCH MOVEMENTS.
BRITISH MOVEMENTS.

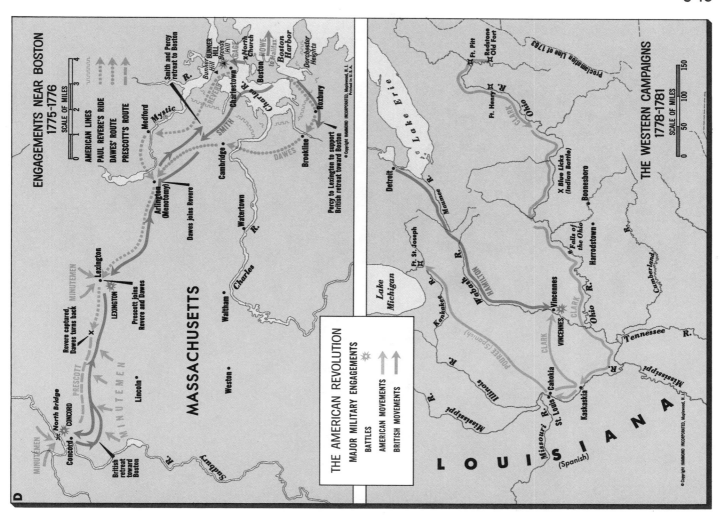

ENGAGEMENTS NEAR BOSTON 1775-1776

SCALE OF MILES
0 1 2 3 4

AMERICAN LINES
PAUL REVERE'S RIDE
DAWES' ROUTE
PRESCOTT'S ROUTE

© Copyright HAMMOND INCORPORATED, Maplewood, N.J. Printed in U.S.A.

Smith and Percy retreat to Boston

BUNKER HILL
Breeds Hill
North Church
Bunker Hill
Charlestown
HOWE
to Halifax
GAGE
Boston
Boston Harbor
Dorchester Heights
Roxbury
Brookline

Percy to Lexington to support British retreat toward Boston

Medford
Mystic R.
SMITH
DAWES
Dawes joins Revere
Arlington (Menotomy)
Cambridge
Watertown
Waltham
Charles R.
Weston

Revere captured, Dawes turns back
X
Prescott joins Revere and Dawes
Lexington
MINUTEMEN

PRESCOTT
Lincoln
MINUTEMEN
North Bridge
CONCORD
Concord
British retreat toward Boston
MINUTEMEN
Sudbury R.

MASSACHUSETTS

THE AMERICAN REVOLUTION
MAJOR MILITARY ENGAGEMENTS

BATTLES
AMERICAN MOVEMENTS
BRITISH MOVEMENTS

THE WESTERN CAMPAIGNS 1778-1781

SCALE OF MILES
0 50 100 150

Lake Erie
Detroit
Ft. Pitt
Redstone Old Fort
CLARK
Ohio R.
Proclamation Line of 1763
Maumee R.
Ft. Henry
X Blue Licks (Indian Battle)
Boonesboro
Falls of the Ohio
Harrodstown
Lake Michigan
Ft. St. Joseph
Wabash R.
HAMILTON
Kaskaskia R.
Vincennes
VINCENNES
CLARK
Ohio R.
Cumberland R.
Tennessee R.
POUTRE (Spanish)
Illinois R.
St. Louis
Cahokia
Kaskaskia
CLARK
Missouri R.
Mississippi R.

LOUISIANA (Spanish)

© Copyright HAMMOND INCORPORATED, Maplewood, N.J.

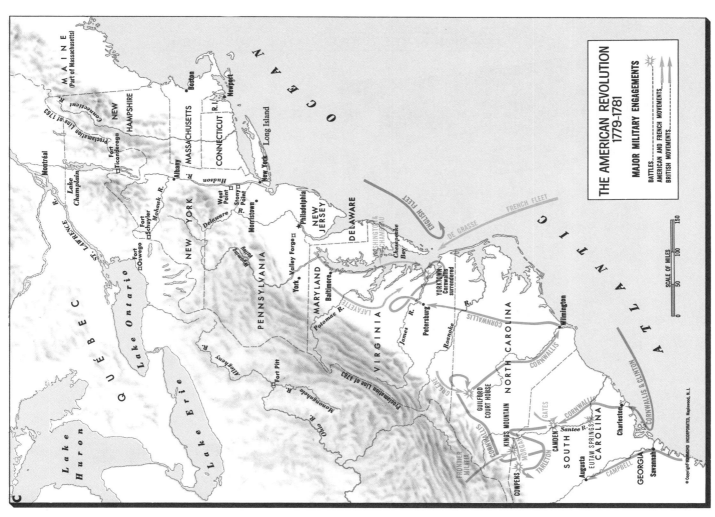

THE AMERICAN REVOLUTION 1779-1781
MAJOR MILITARY ENGAGEMENTS

BATTLES
AMERICAN AND FRENCH MOVEMENTS
BRITISH MOVEMENTS

SCALE OF MILES
0 50 100 150

Lake Huron
Lake Erie
Lake Ontario
QUÉBEC
Montréal
ST. LAWRENCE R.
Lake Champlain
Fort Ticonderoga
MAINE (Part of Massachusetts)
Boston
NEW HAMPSHIRE
MASSACHUSETTS
Proclamation Line of 1763
Connecticut R.
R.I.
CONNECTICUT
Newport
Long Island
New York
Fort Oswego
NEW YORK
Albany
Hudson R.
Mohawk R.
Fort Schuyler
West Point
Stony Point
Susquehanna R.
PENNSYLVANIA
Morristown
NEW JERSEY
Philadelphia
Delaware R.
Valley Forge
DELAWARE
York
MARYLAND
Baltimore
Allegheny R.
Fort Pitt
Monongahela R.
Proclamation Line of 1763
Potomac R.
VIRGINIA
James R.
Petersburg
Roanoke R.
Chesapeake Bay
WASHINGTON
ROCHAMBEAU
ENGLISH FLEET
FRENCH FLEET
DE GRASSE
LAFAYETTE
YORKTOWN Cornwallis surrendered
CORNWALLIS
Wilmington
NORTH CAROLINA
GREENE
GUILFORD COURT HOUSE
CORNWALLIS
GATES
KINGS MOUNTAIN
MORGAN
CAMDEN
Santee R.
EUTAW SPRINGS
SOUTH CAROLINA
FRONTIER MILITIA
COWPENS
TARLETON
CORNWALLIS
Charleston
CORNWALLIS & CLINTON
Augusta
CAMPBELL
GEORGIA
Savannah
ATLANTIC OCEAN

© Copyright HAMMOND INCORPORATED, Maplewood, N.J.

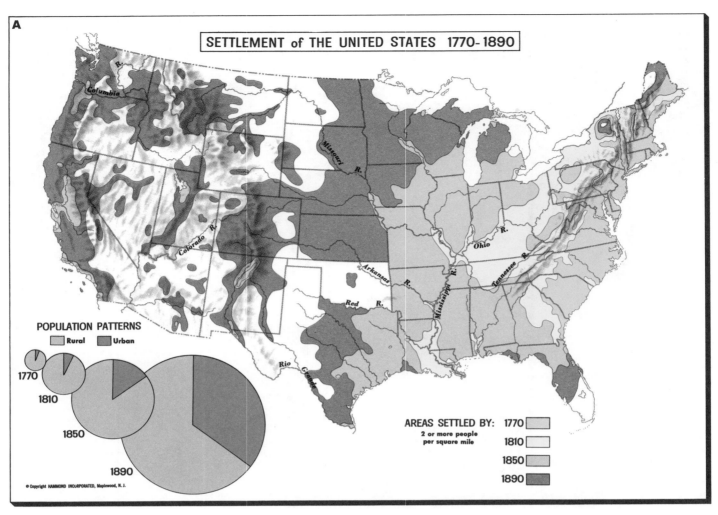

A

SETTLEMENT of THE UNITED STATES 1770-1890

POPULATION PATTERNS

Rural   Urban

1770
1810
1850
1890

AREAS SETTLED BY: 1770
2 or more people per square mile   1810
1850
1890

© Copyright HAMMOND INCORPORATED, Maplewood, N.J.

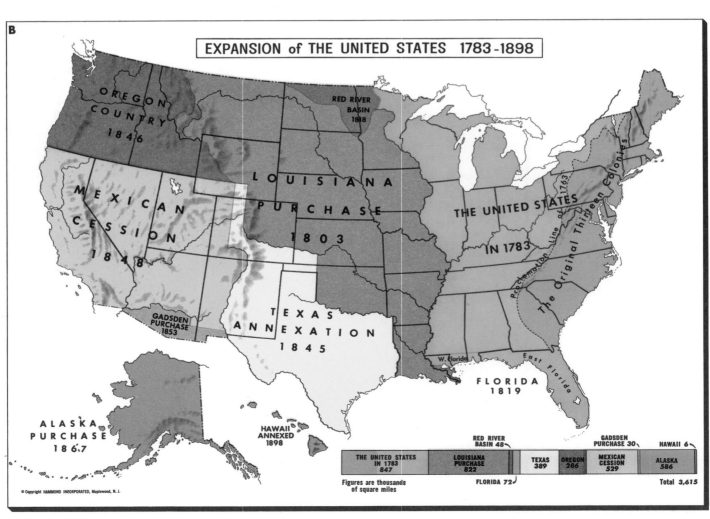

B

EXPANSION of THE UNITED STATES 1783-1898

OREGON COUNTRY 1846

RED RIVER BASIN 1818

MEXICAN CESSION 1848

LOUISIANA PURCHASE 1803

THE UNITED STATES IN 1783

The Original Thirteen Colonies

Proclamation Line of 1763

GADSDEN PURCHASE 1853

TEXAS ANNEXATION 1845

W. Florida   East Florida

FLORIDA 1819

ALASKA PURCHASE 1867

HAWAII ANNEXED 1898

THE UNITED STATES IN 1783 847	LOUISIANA PURCHASE 822	TEXAS 389	OREGON 286	MEXICAN CESSION 529	ALASKA 586

RED RIVER BASIN 48
GADSDEN PURCHASE 30
HAWAII 6
FLORIDA 72

Figures are thousands of square miles

Total 3,615

© Copyright HAMMOND INCORPORATED, Maplewood, N.J.

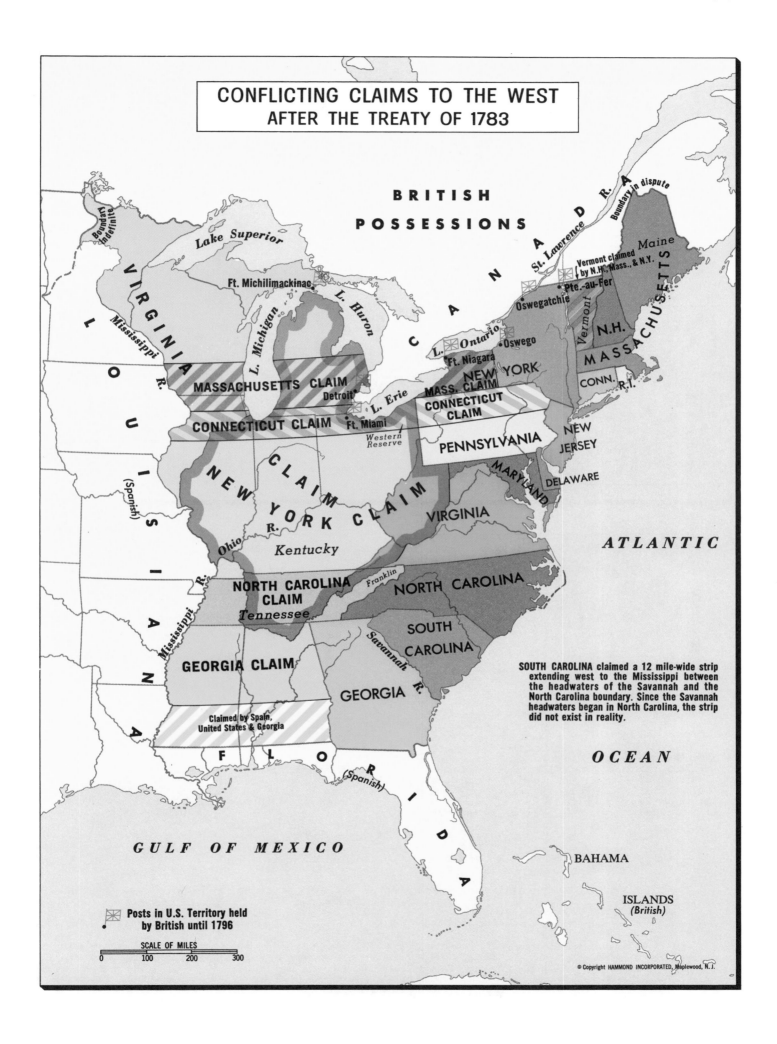

CONFLICTING CLAIMS TO THE WEST AFTER THE TREATY OF 1783

BRITISH POSSESSIONS

CANADA

Boundary in dispute

Lake Superior

Ft. Michilimackinac

L. Huron

L. Michigan

St. Lawrence R.

Maine

Vermont claimed by N.H., Mass., & N.Y.

Pte.-au-Fer

Oswegatchie

VIRGINIA

Mississippi R.

MASSACHUSETTS CLAIM

Detroit

L. Erie

Ft. Miami

Western Reserve

CONNECTICUT CLAIM

L. Ontario

Oswego

Ft. Niagara

MASS. CLAIM

NEW YORK

Vermont

N.H.

MASSACHUSETTS

CONN.

R.I.

CONNECTICUT CLAIM

PENNSYLVANIA

NEW JERSEY

DELAWARE

MARYLAND

NEW YORK CLAIM

Ohio R.

Kentucky

VIRGINIA

ATLANTIC

L O U I S I A N A

(Spanish)

Mississippi R.

NORTH CAROLINA CLAIM

Tennessee

Franklin

NORTH CAROLINA

SOUTH CAROLINA

GEORGIA CLAIM

Savannah R.

GEORGIA

Claimed by Spain, United States & Georgia

F L O R I D A

(Spanish)

SOUTH CAROLINA claimed a 12 mile-wide strip extending west to the Mississippi between the headwaters of the Savannah and the North Carolina boundary. Since the Savannah headwaters began in North Carolina, the strip did not exist in reality.

OCEAN

GULF OF MEXICO

BAHAMA

ISLANDS (British)

Boundary undefinite

⊠ Posts in U.S. Territory held by British until 1796

SCALE OF MILES
0   100   200   300

© Copyright HAMMOND INCORPORATED, Maplewood, N.J.

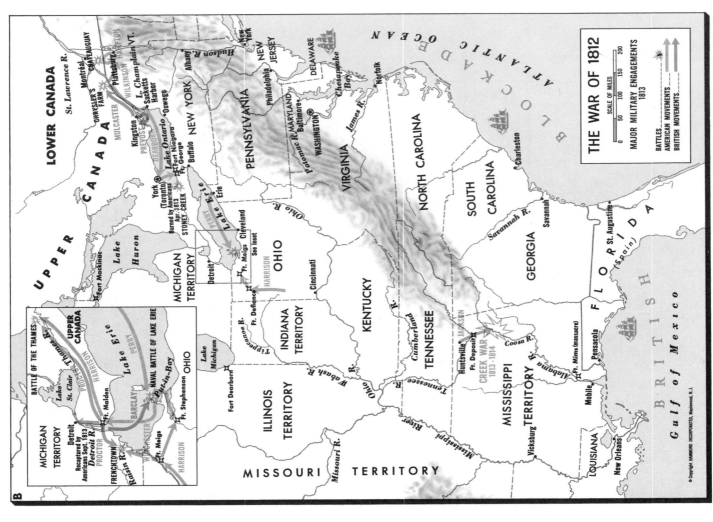

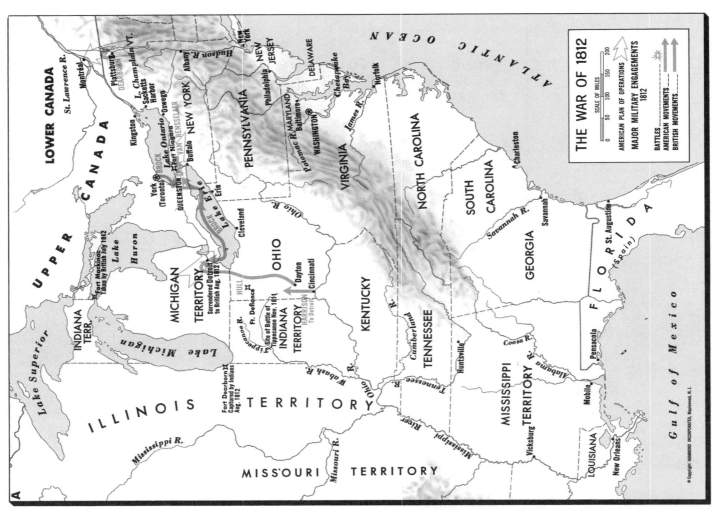

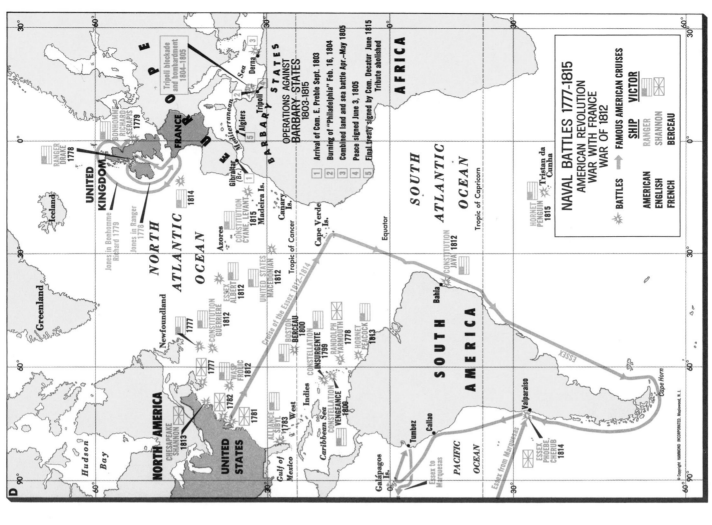

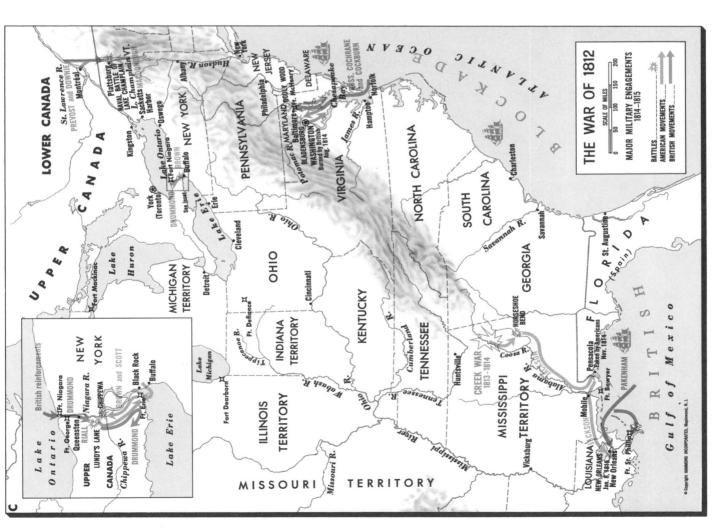

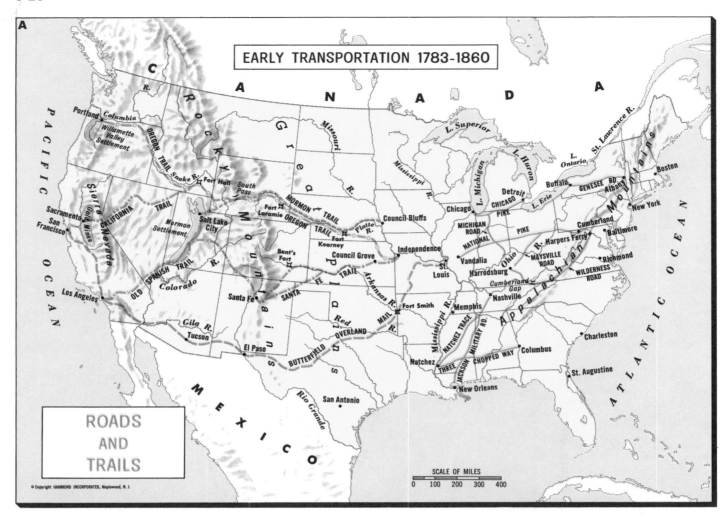

EARLY TRANSPORTATION 1783-1860

ROADS
AND
TRAILS

© Copyright HAMMOND INCORPORATED, Maplewood, N.J.

SCALE OF MILES
0 100 200 300 400

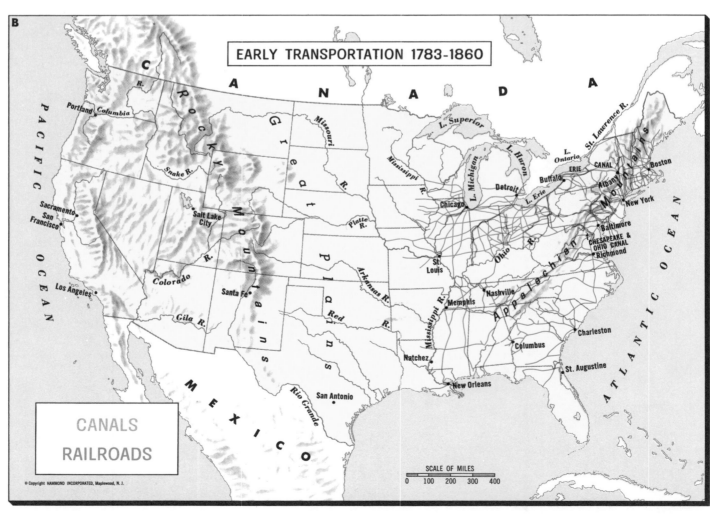

EARLY TRANSPORTATION 1783-1860

CANALS
RAILROADS

© Copyright HAMMOND INCORPORATED, Maplewood, N.J.

SCALE OF MILES
0 100 200 300 400

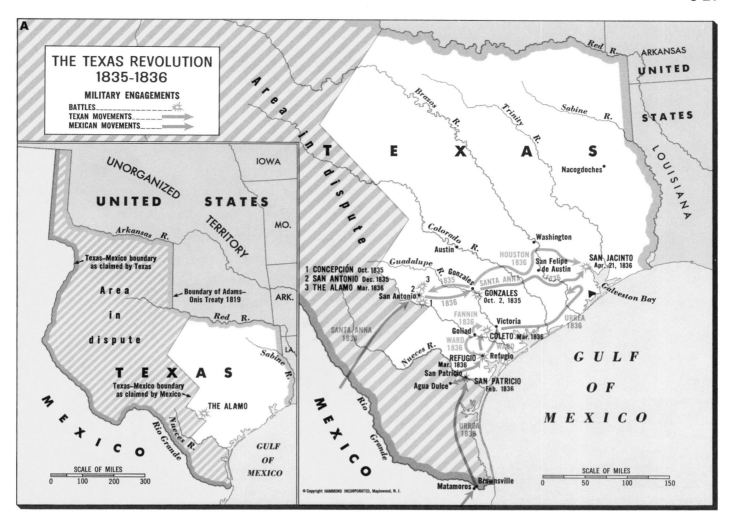

A

THE TEXAS REVOLUTION
1835-1836

MILITARY ENGAGEMENTS
BATTLES
TEXAN MOVEMENTS
MEXICAN MOVEMENTS

UNORGANIZED

UNITED STATES TERRITORY

IOWA

MO.

Arkansas R.

Texas–Mexico boundary
as claimed by Texas

Area
in
dispute

Boundary of Adams–
Onis Treaty 1819

ARK.

Red R.

Sabine R.

LA.

T E X A S

Texas–Mexico boundary
as claimed by Mexico

THE ALAMO

MEXICO

Nueces R.

Rio Grande

GULF
OF
MEXICO

SCALE OF MILES
0   100   200   300

Area in dispute

Red R.

ARKANSAS

UNITED

STATES

T E X A S

Brazos R.

Trinity R.

Sabine R.

Nacogdoches

LOUISIANA

Colorado R.

Washington

Austin

Guadalupe R.

Gonzales

HOUSTON 1836

San Felipe
de Austin

SAN JACINTO
Apr. 21, 1836

1 CONCEPCIÓN Oct. 1835
2 SAN ANTONIO Dec. 1835
3 THE ALAMO Mar. 1836

SANTA ANNA
1836

Galveston Bay

San Antonio

GONZALES
Oct. 2, 1835

SANTA ANNA
1836

FANNIN
1836

Victoria

URREA
1836

Goliad

COLETO Mar. 1836

WARD
1836

G U L F

Nueces R.

REFUGIO
Mar. 1836

Refugio

O F

San Patricio

SAN PATRICIO
Feb. 1836

M E X I C O

Agua Dulce

Rio Grande

URREA
1836

Matamoros

Brownsville

SCALE OF MILES
0   50   100   150

© Copyright HAMMOND INCORPORATED, Maplewood, N.J.

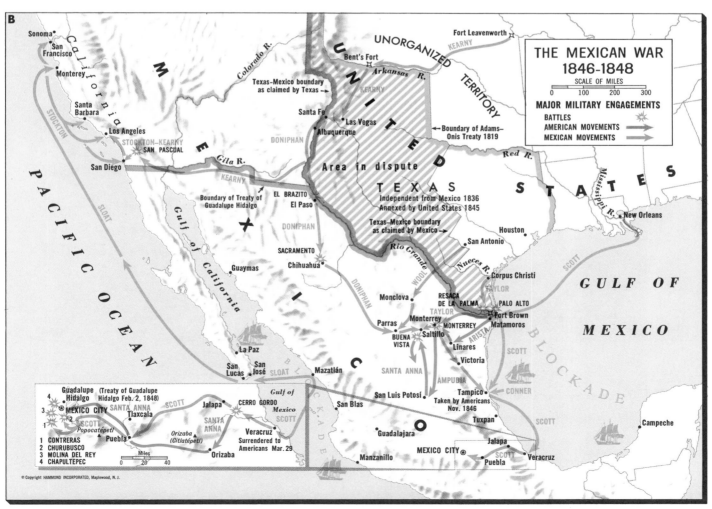

B

Sonoma

San
Francisco

California

Monterey

Santa
Barbara

Los Angeles

STOCKTON–KEARNY
SAN PASCUAL

San Diego

P A C I F I C   O C E A N

SLOAT

STOCKTON

Colorado R.

UNORGANIZED

Fort Leavenworth

KEARNY

THE MEXICAN WAR
1846-1848

SCALE OF MILES
0   100   200   300

MAJOR MILITARY ENGAGEMENTS
BATTLES
AMERICAN MOVEMENTS
MEXICAN MOVEMENTS

Bent's Fort

Arkansas R.

KEARNY

TERRITORY

Santa Fe

Las Vegas

Albuquerque

DONIPHAN

Boundary of Adams–
Onis Treaty 1819

Red R.

U N I T E D

Area in dispute

Texas–Mexico boundary
as claimed by Texas

M

Gila R.

KEARNY

Boundary of Treaty of
Guadalupe Hidalgo

EL BRAZITO
El Paso

DONIPHAN

SACRAMENTO

Chihuahua

Gulf of California

Guaymas

E

T E X A S

Independent from Mexico 1836
Annexed by United States 1845

Texas–Mexico boundary
as claimed by Mexico

Rio Grande

WOOL

Nueces R.

Houston

San Antonio

Corpus Christi

S   T   A   T   E   S

Mississippi R.

New Orleans

G U L F   O F

X

La Paz

San
Lucas

San
José

Mazatlán

SLOAT

I

Monclova

Parras

Monterrey

RESACA
DE LA PALMA

MONTERREY

PALO ALTO

Fort Brown

Matamoros

ARISTA

M E X I C O

BLOCKADE

BUENA
VISTA

Saltillo

Linares

Victoria

SANTA ANNA

AMPUDIA

San Luis Potosí

Tampico
Taken by Americans
Nov. 1846

CONNER

San Blas

Tuxpan

SCOTT

C

Guadalajara

MEXICO CITY

Manzanillo

O

Jalapa

SCOTT

Veracruz

Campeche

1 CONTRERAS
2 CHURUBUSCO
3 MOLINA DEL REY
4 CHAPULTEPEC

Guadalupe
Hidalgo

(Treaty of Guadalupe
Hidalgo Feb. 2, 1848)

SANTA ANNA

MEXICO CITY

Tlaxcala

Popocatépetl

Puebla

SCOTT

Jalapa

CERRO GORDO

SANTA
ANNA

Orizaba
(Citlatépetl)

Gulf of
Mexico

Veracruz
Surrendered to
Americans Mar. 29

Orizaba

SCOTT

BLOCKADE

Miles
0   20   40

© Copyright HAMMOND INCORPORATED, Maplewood, N.J.

A

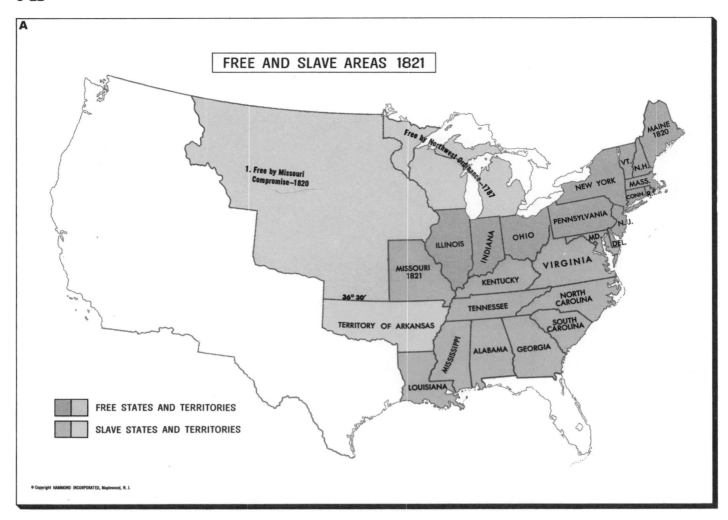

FREE AND SLAVE AREAS 1821

Free by Northwest Ordinance–1787

1. Free by Missouri Compromise–1820

MAINE 1820

VT.

N.H.

NEW YORK

MASS.

CONN. R.I.

PENNSYLVANIA

N.J.

ILLINOIS

INDIANA

OHIO

MD

DEL.

MISSOURI 1821

VIRGINIA

KENTUCKY

36° 30'

TENNESSEE

NORTH CAROLINA

TERRITORY OF ARKANSAS

SOUTH CAROLINA

MISSISSIPPI

ALABAMA

GEORGIA

LOUISIANA

☐☐ FREE STATES AND TERRITORIES

☐☐ SLAVE STATES AND TERRITORIES

© Copyright HAMMOND INCORPORATED, Maplewood, N.J.

B

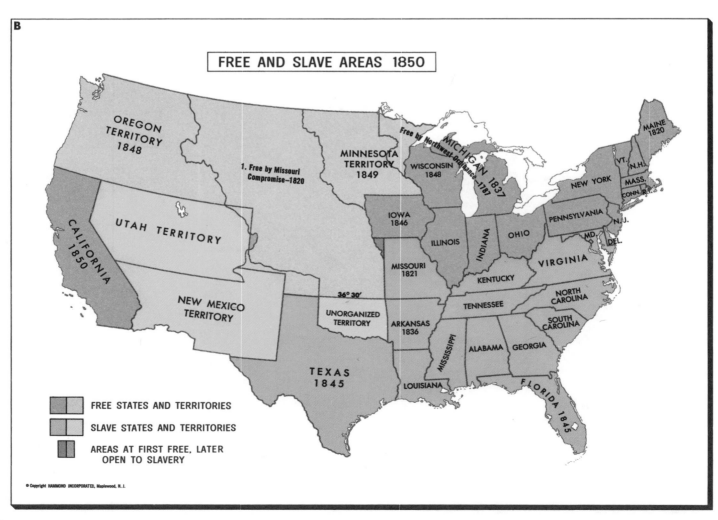

FREE AND SLAVE AREAS 1850

OREGON TERRITORY 1848

Free by Northwest Ordinance–1787

MICHIGAN 1837

MINNESOTA TERRITORY 1849

WISCONSIN 1848

MAINE 1820

1. Free by Missouri Compromise–1820

VT.

N.H.

NEW YORK

MASS.

CONN. R.I.

UTAH TERRITORY

IOWA 1846

PENNSYLVANIA

N.J.

CALIFORNIA 1850

ILLINOIS

INDIANA

OHIO

MD

DEL.

MISSOURI 1821

VIRGINIA

KENTUCKY

NEW MEXICO TERRITORY

36° 30'

TENNESSEE

NORTH CAROLINA

UNORGANIZED TERRITORY

ARKANSAS 1836

SOUTH CAROLINA

MISSISSIPPI

ALABAMA

GEORGIA

TEXAS 1845

LOUISIANA

FLORIDA 1845

☐☐ FREE STATES AND TERRITORIES

☐☐ SLAVE STATES AND TERRITORIES

☐☐ AREAS AT FIRST FREE, LATER OPEN TO SLAVERY

© Copyright HAMMOND INCORPORATED, Maplewood, N.J.

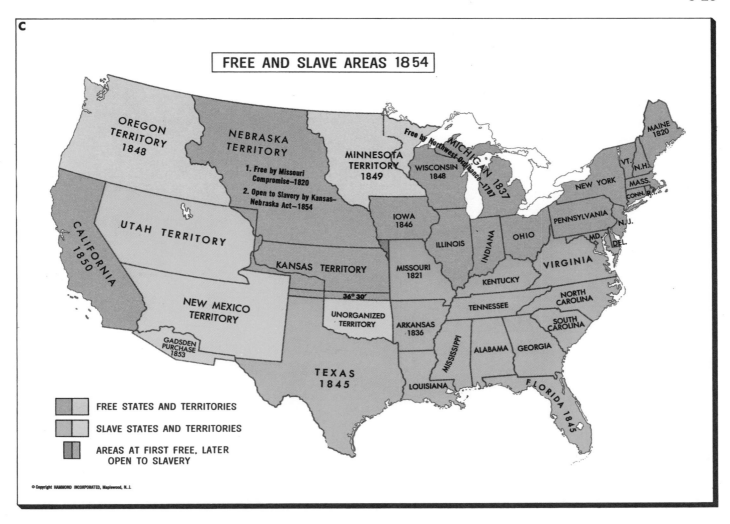

C

FREE AND SLAVE AREAS 1854

OREGON TERRITORY 1848

NEBRASKA TERRITORY

1. Free by Missouri Compromise–1820
2. Open to Slavery by Kansas–Nebraska Act–1854

MINNESOTA TERRITORY 1849

Free by Northwest Ordinance–1787

MICHIGAN 1837

WISCONSIN 1848

NEW YORK

MAINE 1820

VT. N.H.

MASS.

CONN. R.I.

UTAH TERRITORY

IOWA 1846

ILLINOIS INDIANA OHIO

PENNSYLVANIA

N.J.

MD. DEL.

CALIFORNIA 1850

KANSAS TERRITORY

MISSOURI 1821

KENTUCKY

VIRGINIA

NEW MEXICO TERRITORY

36° 30'

UNORGANIZED TERRITORY

TENNESSEE

NORTH CAROLINA

GADSDEN PURCHASE 1853

ARKANSAS 1836

SOUTH CAROLINA

MISSISSIPPI ALABAMA GEORGIA

TEXAS 1845

LOUISIANA

FLORIDA 1845

FREE STATES AND TERRITORIES

SLAVE STATES AND TERRITORIES

AREAS AT FIRST FREE, LATER OPEN TO SLAVERY

© Copyright HAMMOND INCORPORATED, Maplewood, N.J.

D

FREE AND SLAVE AREAS 1861
at the outbreak of the Civil War

WASHINGTON TERRITORY

OREGON 1859

DAKOTA TERRITORY

MINNESOTA 1858

MAINE

WISCONSIN

MICHIGAN

NEW YORK

VT. N.H.

MASS.

CONN. R.I.

NEVADA TERRITORY

UTAH TERRITORY

NEBRASKA TERRITORY

IOWA

PENNSYLVANIA

N.J.

MASON-DIXON LINE

MD. DEL.

CALIFORNIA

COLORADO TERRITORY

ILLINOIS INDIANA OHIO

KANSAS 1861

MISSOURI

KENTUCKY

VIRGINIA

PUBLIC LAND

NEW MEXICO TERRITORY

INDIAN TERRITORY

ARKANSAS

TENNESSEE

NORTH CAROLINA

SOUTH CAROLINA

MISSISSIPPI ALABAMA GEORGIA

TEXAS

LOUISIANA

FLORIDA

FREE STATES

SLAVE STATES

TERRITORIES OPEN TO SLAVERY BY DRED SCOTT DECISION 1857

© Copyright HAMMOND INCORPORATED, Maplewood, N.J.

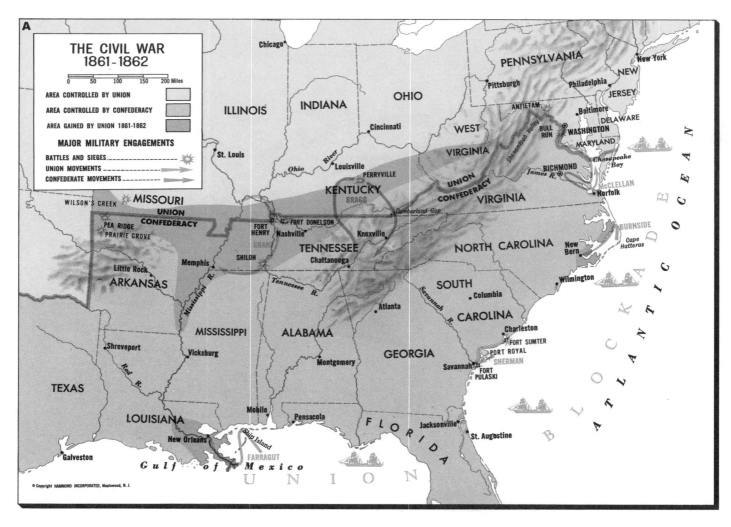

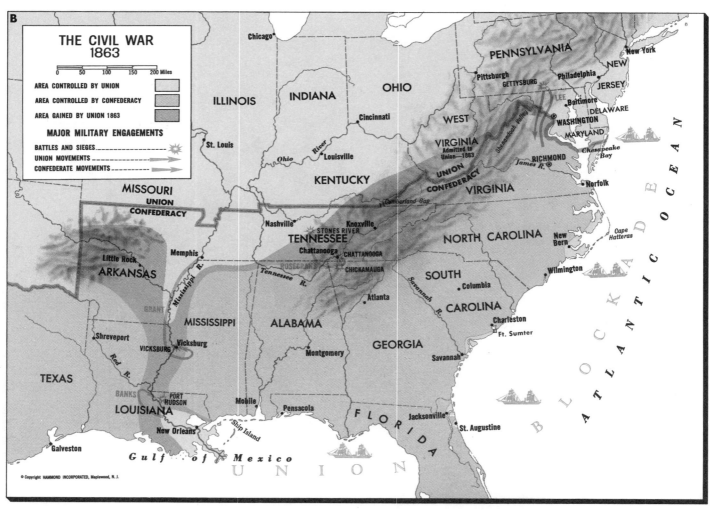

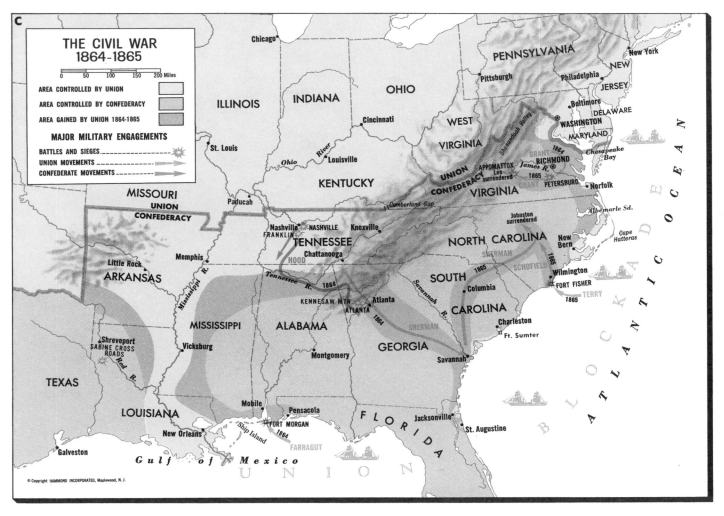

C

THE CIVIL WAR
1864-1865

0   50   100   150   200 Miles

AREA CONTROLLED BY UNION

AREA CONTROLLED BY CONFEDERACY

AREA GAINED BY UNION 1864-1865

MAJOR MILITARY ENGAGEMENTS

BATTLES AND SIEGES

UNION MOVEMENTS

CONFEDERATE MOVEMENTS

© Copyright HAMMOND INCORPORATED, Maplewood, N. J.

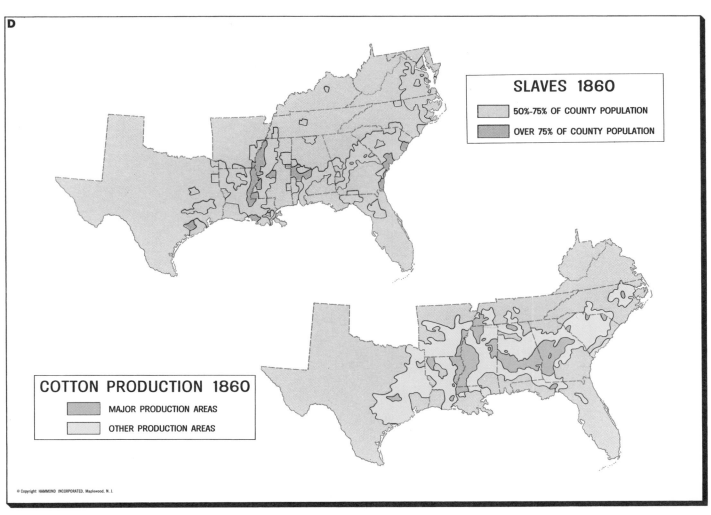

D

SLAVES 1860

50%-75% OF COUNTY POPULATION

OVER 75% OF COUNTY POPULATION

COTTON PRODUCTION 1860

MAJOR PRODUCTION AREAS

OTHER PRODUCTION AREAS

© Copyright HAMMOND INCORPORATED, Maplewood, N. J.

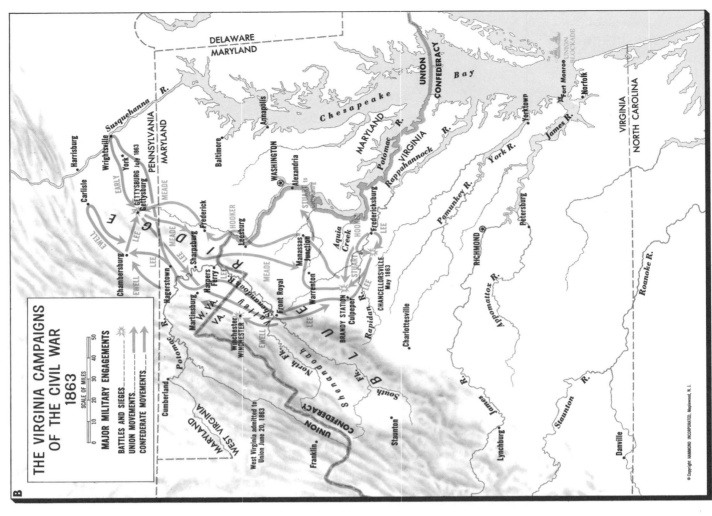

THE VIRGINIA CAMPAIGNS OF THE CIVIL WAR 1863

SCALE OF MILES
0 10 20 30 40 50

MAJOR MILITARY ENGAGEMENTS

BATTLES AND SIEGES
UNION MOVEMENTS
CONFEDERATE MOVEMENTS

West Virginia admitted to Union June 20, 1863

© Copyright HAMMOND INCORPORATED, Maplewood, N.J.

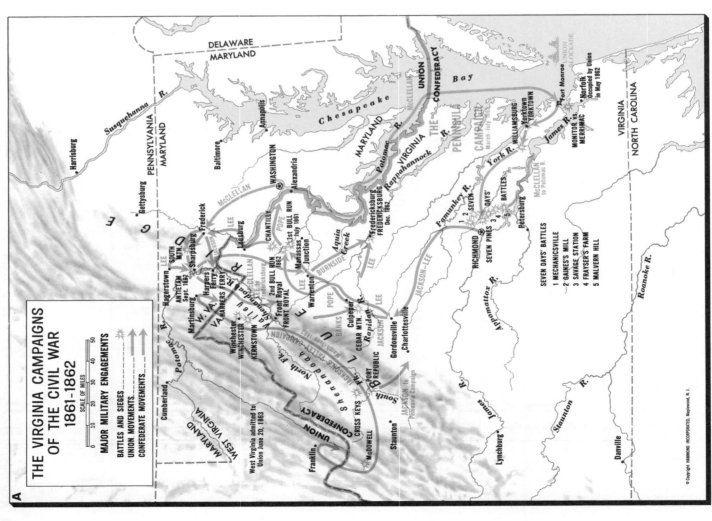

THE VIRGINIA CAMPAIGNS OF THE CIVIL WAR 1861-1862

SCALE OF MILES
0 10 20 30 40 50

MAJOR MILITARY ENGAGEMENTS

BATTLES AND SIEGES
UNION MOVEMENTS
CONFEDERATE MOVEMENTS

West Virginia admitted to Union June 20, 1863

SEVEN DAYS' BATTLES

1 MECHANICSVILLE
2 GAINES'S MILL
3 SAVAGE STATION
4 FRAYSER'S FARM
5 MALVERN HILL

© Copyright HAMMOND INCORPORATED, Maplewood, N.J.

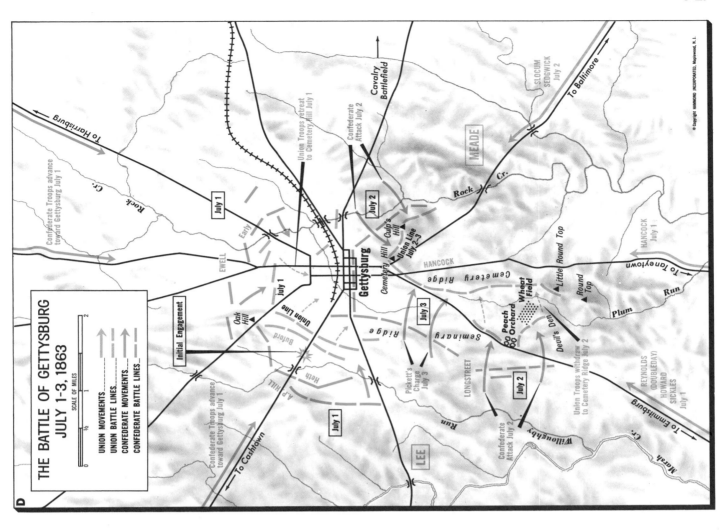

THE BATTLE OF GETTYSBURG
JULY 1-3, 1863

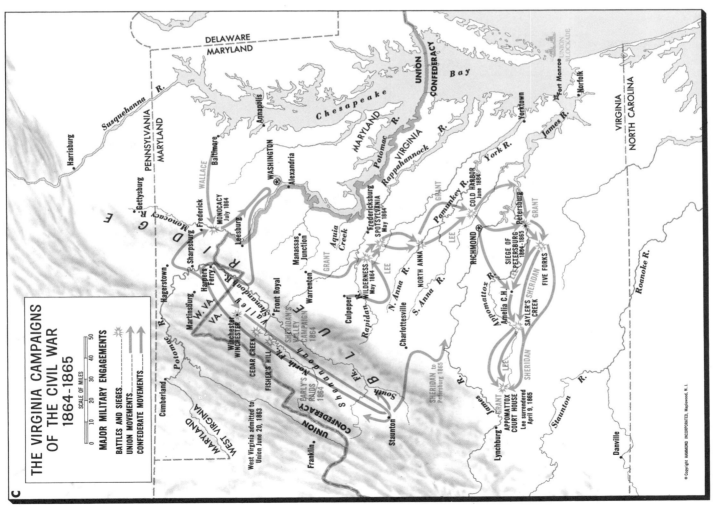

THE VIRGINIA CAMPAIGNS
OF THE CIVIL WAR
1864-1865

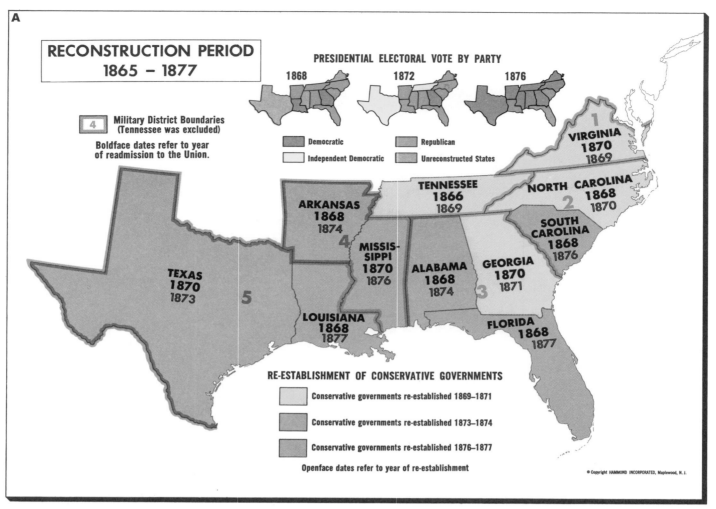

RECONSTRUCTION PERIOD 1865 – 1877

PRESIDENTIAL ELECTORAL VOTE BY PARTY

1868   1872   1876

☐ 4 Military District Boundaries (Tennessee was excluded)

Boldface dates refer to year of readmission to the Union.

- Democratic
- Independent Democratic
- Republican
- Unreconstructed States

VIRGINIA 1870 *1869*

TENNESSEE 1866 *1869*

NORTH CAROLINA 1868 *1870*

ARKANSAS 1868 *1874*

SOUTH CAROLINA 1868 *1876*

MISSISSIPPI 1870 *1876*

ALABAMA 1868 *1874*

GEORGIA 1870 *1871*

TEXAS 1870 *1873*

LOUISIANA 1868 *1877*

FLORIDA 1868 *1877*

RE-ESTABLISHMENT OF CONSERVATIVE GOVERNMENTS

- Conservative governments re-established 1869–1871
- Conservative governments re-established 1873–1874
- Conservative governments re-established 1876–1877

Openface dates refer to year of re-establishment

© Copyright HAMMOND INCORPORATED, Maplewood, N.J.

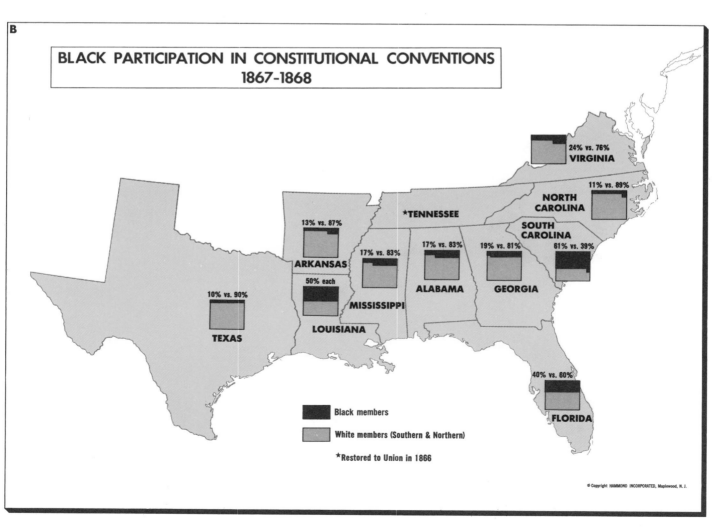

BLACK PARTICIPATION IN CONSTITUTIONAL CONVENTIONS 1867-1868

24% vs. 76% VIRGINIA

11% vs. 89% NORTH CAROLINA

*TENNESSEE

SOUTH CAROLINA 61% vs. 39%

13% vs. 87% ARKANSAS

17% vs. 83% MISSISSIPPI

17% vs. 83% ALABAMA

19% vs. 81% GEORGIA

50% each LOUISIANA

10% vs. 90% TEXAS

40% vs. 60% FLORIDA

- Black members
- White members (Southern & Northern)

*Restored to Union in 1866

© Copyright HAMMOND INCORPORATED, Maplewood, N.J.

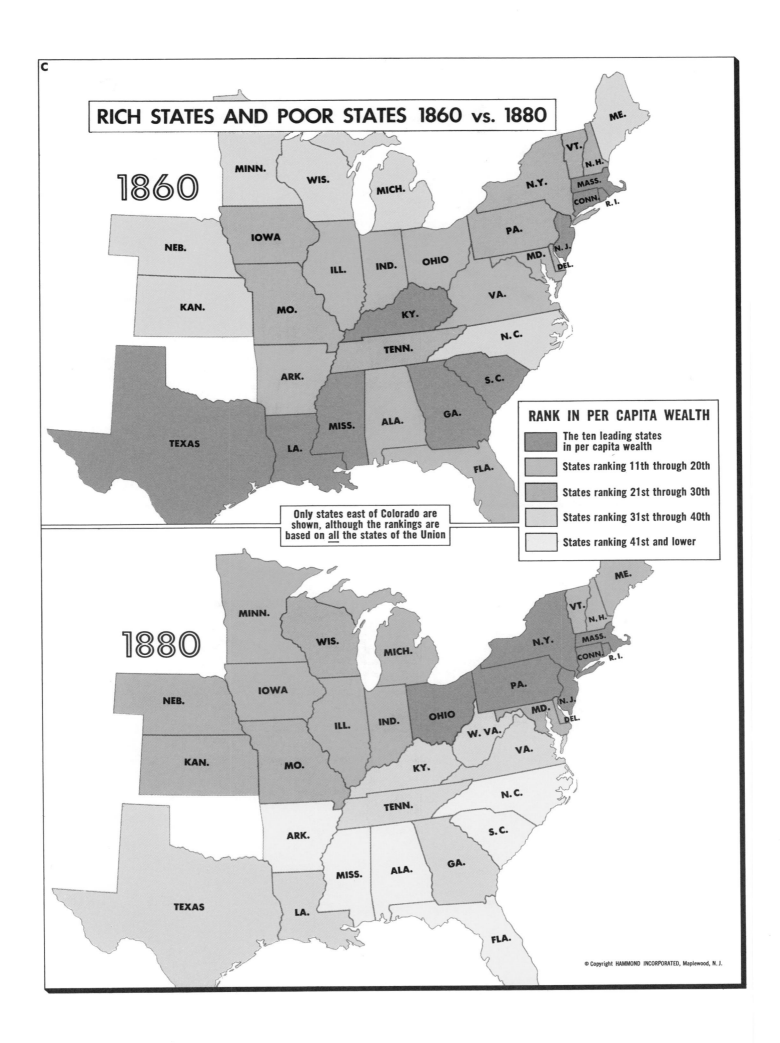

RICH STATES AND POOR STATES 1860 vs. 1880

1860

1880

Only states east of Colorado are shown, although the rankings are based on all the states of the Union

RANK IN PER CAPITA WEALTH

The ten leading states in per capita wealth

States ranking 11th through 20th

States ranking 21st through 30th

States ranking 31st through 40th

States ranking 41st and lower

© Copyright HAMMOND INCORPORATED, Maplewood, N. J.

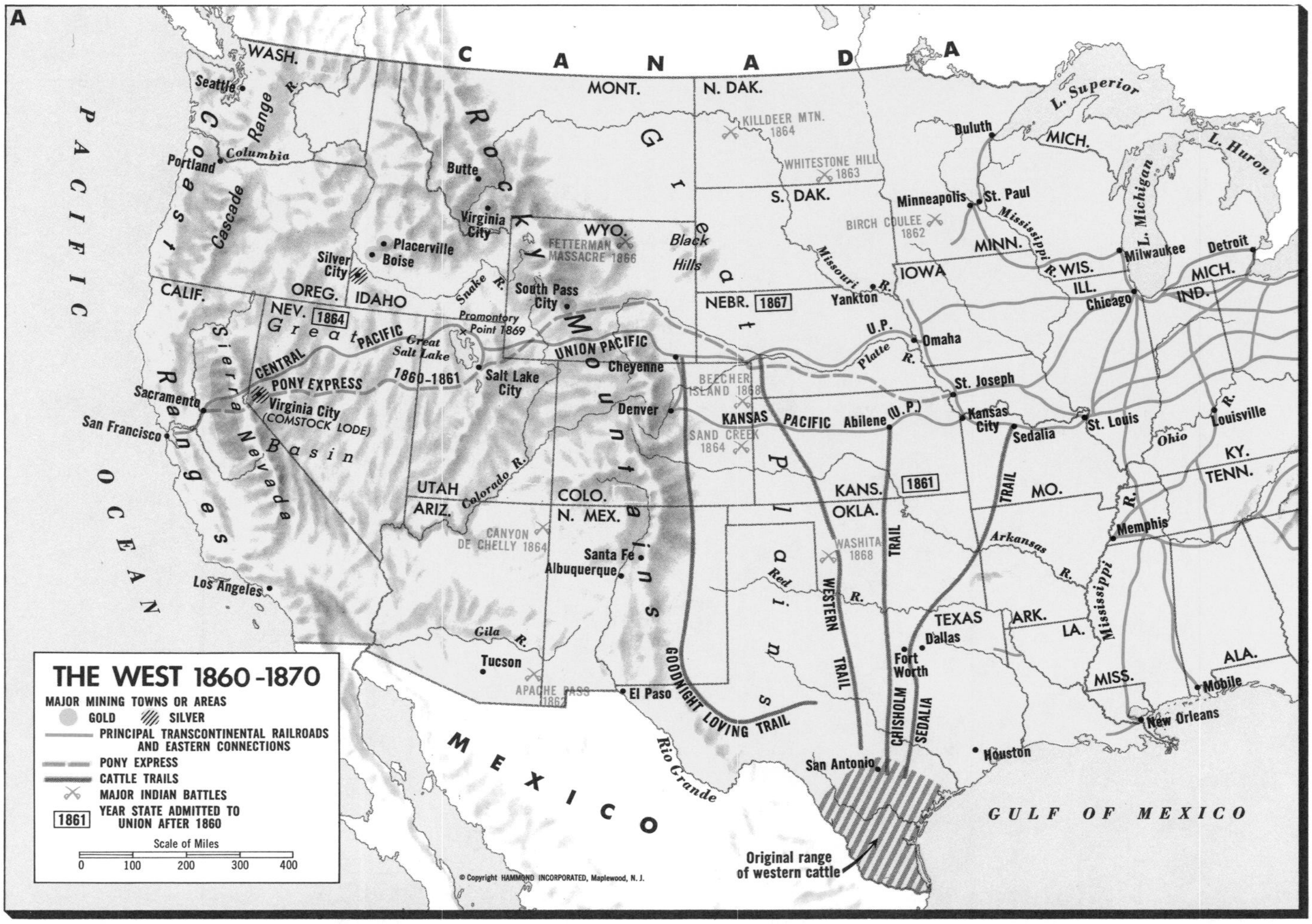
A
THE WEST 1860-1870
MAJOR MINING TOWNS OR AREAS
GOLD
SILVER
PRINCIPAL TRANSCONTINENTAL RAILROADS AND EASTERN CONNECTIONS
PONY EXPRESS
CATTLE TRAILS
MAJOR INDIAN BATTLES
1861
YEAR STATE ADMITTED TO UNION AFTER 1860
Scale of Miles
0
100
200
300
400
CANADA
PACIFIC OCEAN
MEXICO
GULF OF MEXICO
WASH.
MONT.
N. DAK.
S. DAK.
WYO.
OREG.
IDAHO
CALIF.
NEV. 1864
UTAH
ARIZ.
COLO.
N. MEX.
NEBR. 1867
KANS. 1861
OKLA.
TEXAS
MINN.
IOWA
MO.
ARK.
LA.
MISS.
ALA.
TENN.
KY.
WIS.
ILL.
IND.
MICH.
Coast Range
Cascade
Sierra Nevada
Ranges
Great Basin
Rocky Mountains
Great Plains
Black Hills
Columbia
Snake R.
Colorado R.
Gila R.
Rio Grande
Red R.
Arkansas R.
Platte R.
Missouri R.
Mississippi R.
Ohio R.
L. Superior
L. Michigan
L. Huron
Great Salt Lake
Seattle
Portland
Butte
Virginia City
Placerville
Boise
Silver City
South Pass City
Promontory Point 1869
Salt Lake City
Sacramento
San Francisco
Virginia City (COMSTOCK LODE)
Los Angeles
Tucson
El Paso
Santa Fe
Albuquerque
Denver
Cheyenne
Yankton
Omaha
St. Joseph
Kansas City
Sedalia
Abilene
Fort Worth
Dallas
San Antonio
Houston
New Orleans
Mobile
Memphis
St. Louis
Louisville
Chicago
Milwaukee
Detroit
Minneapolis
St. Paul
Duluth
CENTRAL PACIFIC
UNION PACIFIC
KANSAS PACIFIC
(U.P.)
PONY EXPRESS 1860-1861
GOODNIGHT LOVING TRAIL
WESTERN TRAIL
CHISHOLM TRAIL
SEDALIA TRAIL
KILLDEER MTN. 1864
WHITESTONE HILL 1863
BIRCH COULEE 1862
FETTERMAN MASSACRE 1866
BEECHER ISLAND 1868
SAND CREEK 1864
WASHITA 1868
CANYON DE CHELLY 1864
APACHE PASS 1862
Original range of western cattle
© Copyright HAMMOND INCORPORATED, Maplewood, N. J.

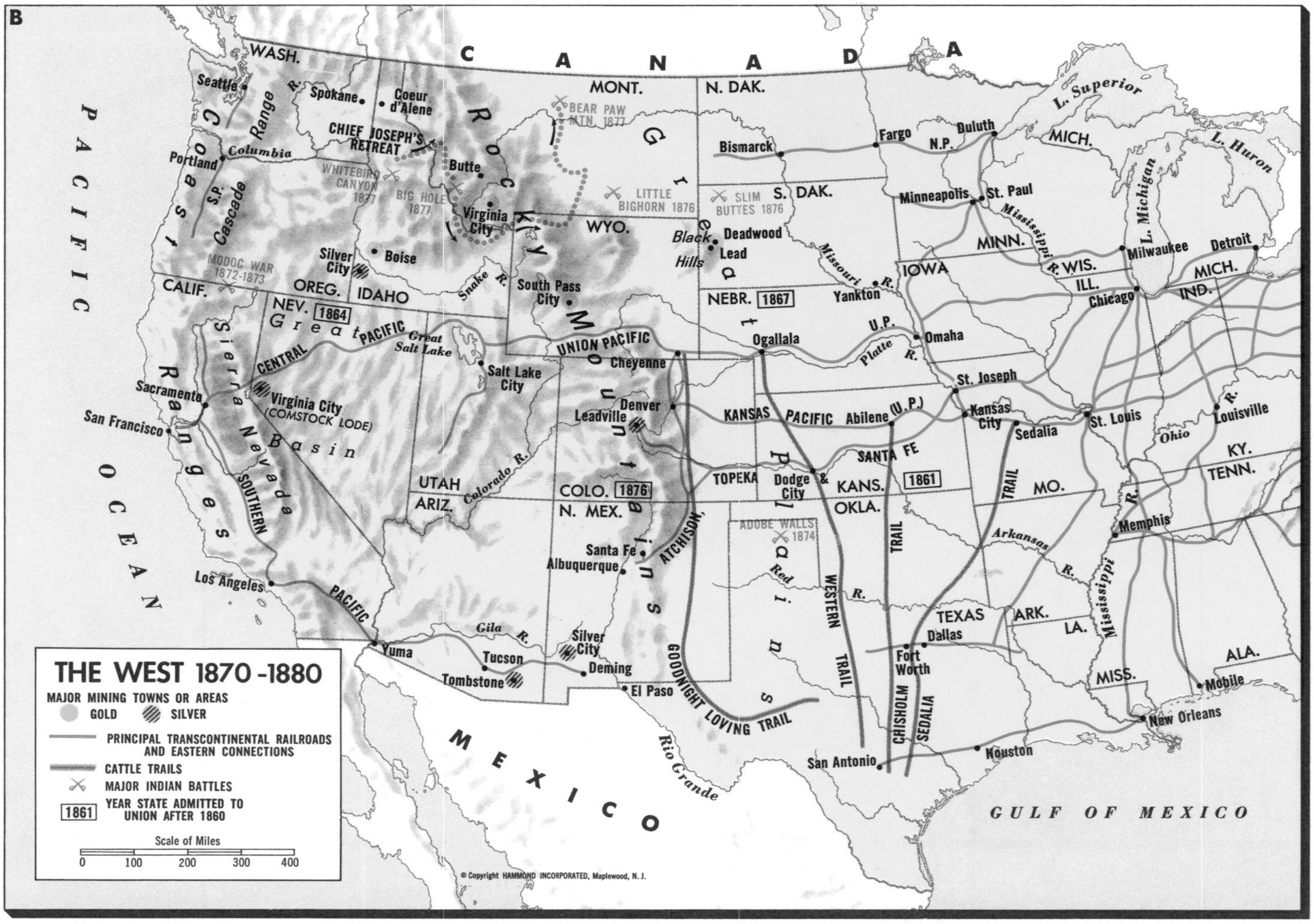
B
THE WEST 1870-1880
MAJOR MINING TOWNS OR AREAS
GOLD
SILVER
PRINCIPAL TRANSCONTINENTAL RAILROADS AND EASTERN CONNECTIONS
CATTLE TRAILS
MAJOR INDIAN BATTLES
1861
YEAR STATE ADMITTED TO UNION AFTER 1860
Scale of Miles
0
100
200
300
400
CANADA
PACIFIC OCEAN
MEXICO
GULF OF MEXICO
WASH.
MONT.
N. DAK.
S. DAK.
WYO.
OREG.
IDAHO
CALIF.
NEV. 1864
UTAH
ARIZ.
COLO. 1876
N. MEX.
NEBR. 1867
KANS. 1861
OKLA.
TEXAS
MINN.
IOWA
MO.
ARK.
LA.
MISS.
ALA.
TENN.
KY.
WIS.
ILL.
IND.
MICH.
Coast Range
Cascade
Sierra Nevada
Ranges
Great Basin
Rocky Mountains
Great Plains
Black Hills
Columbia
Snake R.
Colorado R.
Gila R.
Rio Grande
Red R.
Arkansas R.
Platte R.
Missouri R.
Mississippi R.
Ohio R.
L. Superior
L. Michigan
L. Huron
Great Salt Lake
Seattle
Spokane
Coeur d'Alene
Portland
Butte
Virginia City
Boise
Silver City
South Pass City
Salt Lake City
Sacramento
San Francisco
Virginia City (COMSTOCK LODE)
Los Angeles
Yuma
Tucson
Tombstone
Silver City
Deming
El Paso
Santa Fe
Albuquerque
Leadville
Denver
Cheyenne
Deadwood
Lead
Bismarck
Fargo
Yankton
Ogallala
Omaha
St. Joseph
Kansas City
Topeka
Dodge City
Sedalia
Abilene
Fort Worth
Dallas
San Antonio
Houston
New Orleans
Mobile
Memphis
St. Louis
Louisville
Chicago
Milwaukee
Detroit
Minneapolis
St. Paul
Duluth
N.P.
S.P.
CENTRAL PACIFIC
UNION PACIFIC
KANSAS PACIFIC
(U.P.)
SOUTHERN PACIFIC
ATCHISON, TOPEKA & SANTA FE
CHIEF JOSEPH'S RETREAT
GOODNIGHT LOVING TRAIL
WESTERN TRAIL
CHISHOLM TRAIL
SEDALIA TRAIL
BEAR PAW MTN. 1877
LITTLE BIGHORN 1876
SLIM BUTTES 1876
WHITEBIRD CANYON 1877
BIG HOLE 1877
MODOC WAR 1872-1873
ADOBE WALLS 1874
© Copyright HAMMOND INCORPORATED, Maplewood, N. J.

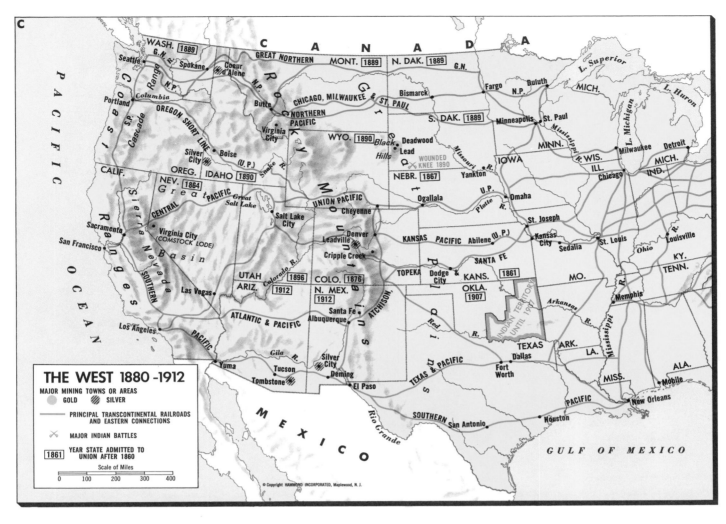

THE WEST 1880-1912

MAJOR MINING TOWNS OR AREAS

- ● GOLD
- ▨ SILVER

—— PRINCIPAL TRANSCONTINENTAL RAILROADS AND EASTERN CONNECTIONS

✕ MAJOR INDIAN BATTLES

1861 YEAR STATE ADMITTED TO UNION AFTER 1860

Scale of Miles
0   100   200   300   400

© Copyright HAMMOND INCORPORATED, Maplewood, N.J.

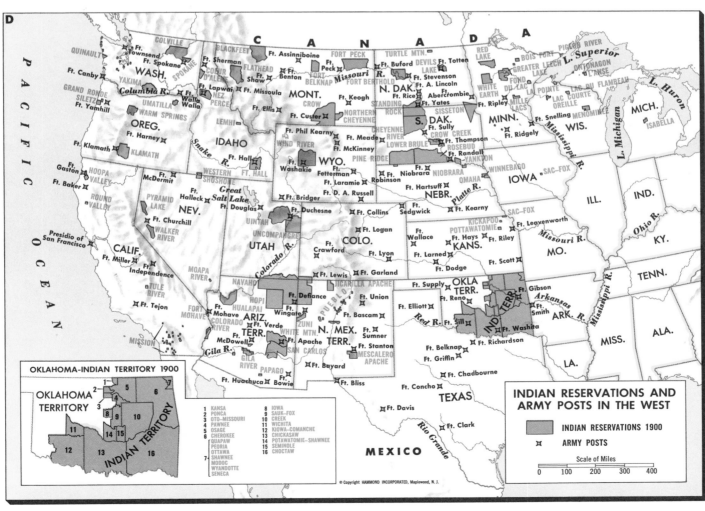

OKLAHOMA-INDIAN TERRITORY 1900

OKLAHOMA TERRITORY

INDIAN TERRITORY

1 KANSA
2 PONCA
3 OTO-MISSOURI
4 PAWNEE
5 OSAGE
6 CHEROKEE
 QUAPAW
 PEORIA
 OTTAWA
7 SHAWNEE
 MODOC
 WYANDOTTE
 SENECA
8 IOWA
9 SAUK-FOX
10 CREEK
11 WICHITA
12 KIOWA-COMANCHE
13 CHICKASAW
14 POTAWATOMIE-SHAWNEE
15 SEMINOLE
16 CHOCTAW

INDIAN RESERVATIONS AND ARMY POSTS IN THE WEST

▨ INDIAN RESERVATIONS 1900

⋈ ARMY POSTS

Scale of Miles
0   100   200   300   400

© Copyright HAMMOND INCORPORATED, Maplewood, N.J.

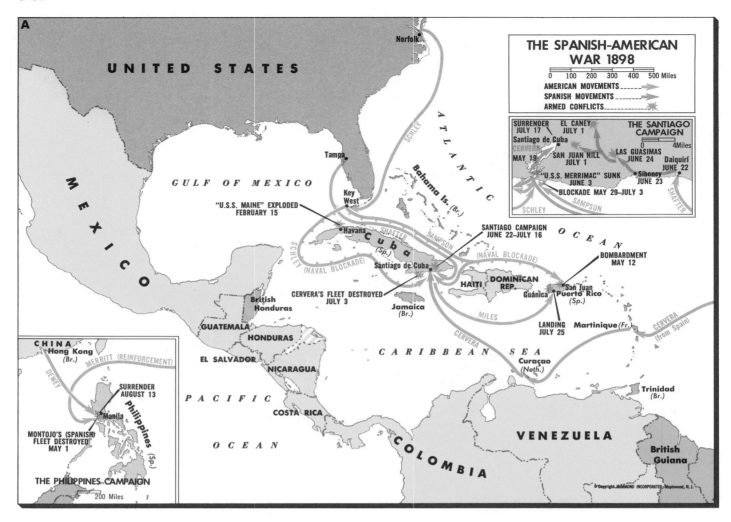

A

THE SPANISH-AMERICAN WAR 1898

0 100 200 300 400 500 Miles

AMERICAN MOVEMENTS
SPANISH MOVEMENTS
ARMED CONFLICTS

THE SANTIAGO CAMPAIGN

SURRENDER JULY 17   EL CANEY JULY 1
Santiago de Cuba
CERVERA MAY 19   SAN JUAN HILL JULY 1   LAS GUASIMAS JUNE 24   Daiquirí JUNE 22
"U.S.S. MERRIMAC" SUNK JUNE 3   Siboney JUNE 23
BLOCKADE MAY 29–JULY 3

0   4 Miles

SCHLEY   SAMPSON   SHAFTER

UNITED STATES

MEXICO

GULF OF MEXICO

Norfolk

Tampa

Key West

"U.S.S. MAINE" EXPLODED FEBRUARY 15

Havana

Cuba (Sp.)

SCHLEY (NAVAL BLOCKADE)

SANTIAGO CAMPAIGN JUNE 22–JULY 16

Santiago de Cuba

CERVERA'S FLEET DESTROYED JULY 3

Jamaica (Br.)

Bahama Is. (Br.)

ATLANTIC OCEAN

(NAVAL BLOCKADE)

HAITI

DOMINICAN REP.

Guánica

San Juan Puerto Rico (Sp.)

BOMBARDMENT MAY 12

LANDING JULY 25

Martinique (Fr.)

MILES

CERVERA

CERVERA (from Spain)

British Honduras

GUATEMALA

HONDURAS

EL SALVADOR

NICARAGUA

COSTA RICA

CARIBBEAN SEA

Curaçao (Neth.)

Trinidad (Br.)

VENEZUELA

COLOMBIA

PACIFIC OCEAN

© Copyright HAMMOND INCORPORATED, Maplewood, N.J.

CHINA
Hong Kong (Br.)

MERRITT (REINFORCEMENT)

DEWEY

SURRENDER AUGUST 13

Manila

Philippines (Sp.)

MONTOJO'S (SPANISH) FLEET DESTROYED MAY 1

PACIFIC OCEAN

THE PHILIPPINES CAMPAIGN

0   200 Miles

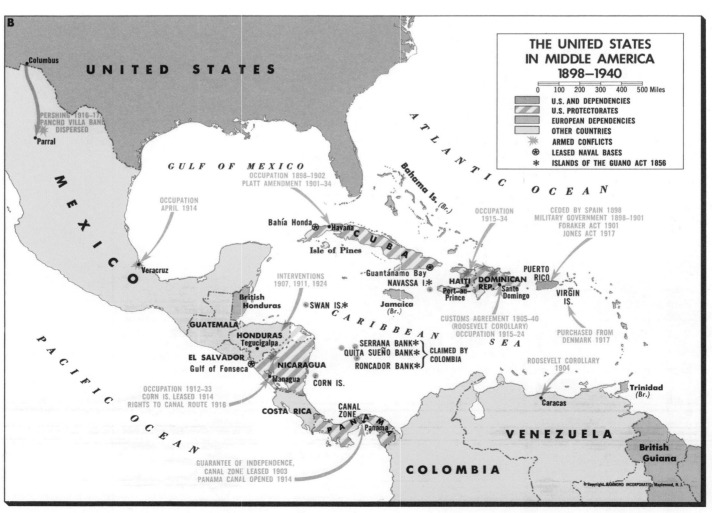

B

THE UNITED STATES IN MIDDLE AMERICA 1898–1940

0 100 200 300 400 500 Miles

U.S. AND DEPENDENCIES
U.S. PROTECTORATES
EUROPEAN DEPENDENCIES
OTHER COUNTRIES
ARMED CONFLICTS
LEASED NAVAL BASES
ISLANDS OF THE GUANO ACT 1856

UNITED STATES

Columbus

PERSHING 1916–17, PANCHO VILLA BAND DISPERSED

Parral

MEXICO

GULF OF MEXICO

OCCUPATION 1898–1902
PLATT AMENDMENT 1901–34

OCCUPATION APRIL 1914

Veracruz

Bahía Honda

Havana

CUBA

Isle of Pines

INTERVENTIONS 1907, 1911, 1924

Bahama Is. (Br.)

ATLANTIC OCEAN

OCCUPATION 1915–34

CEDED BY SPAIN 1898
MILITARY GOVERNMENT 1898–1901
FORAKER ACT 1901
JONES ACT 1917

Guantánamo Bay
NAVASSA I.*

HAITI
Port-au-Prince

DOMINICAN REP.
Santo Domingo

PUERTO RICO

VIRGIN IS.

Jamaica (Br.)

SWAN IS.*

British Honduras

GUATEMALA

HONDURAS
Tegucigalpa

EL SALVADOR
Gulf of Fonseca

NICARAGUA
Managua

CORN IS.

OCCUPATION 1912–33
CORN IS. LEASED 1914
RIGHTS TO CANAL ROUTE 1916

COSTA RICA

CANAL ZONE
PANAMA
Panama

CARIBBEAN SEA

SERRANA BANK*
QUITA SUEÑO BANK*
RONCADOR BANK*

CLAIMED BY COLOMBIA

CUSTOMS AGREEMENT 1905–40
(ROOSEVELT COROLLARY)
OCCUPATION 1915–24

PURCHASED FROM DENMARK 1917

ROOSEVELT COROLLARY 1904

PURCHASED FROM DENMARK 1917

Trinidad (Br.)

Caracas

VENEZUELA

COLOMBIA

GUARANTEE OF INDEPENDENCE, CANAL ZONE LEASED 1903
PANAMA CANAL OPENED 1914

PACIFIC OCEAN

British Guiana

© Copyright HAMMOND INCORPORATED, Maplewood, N.J.

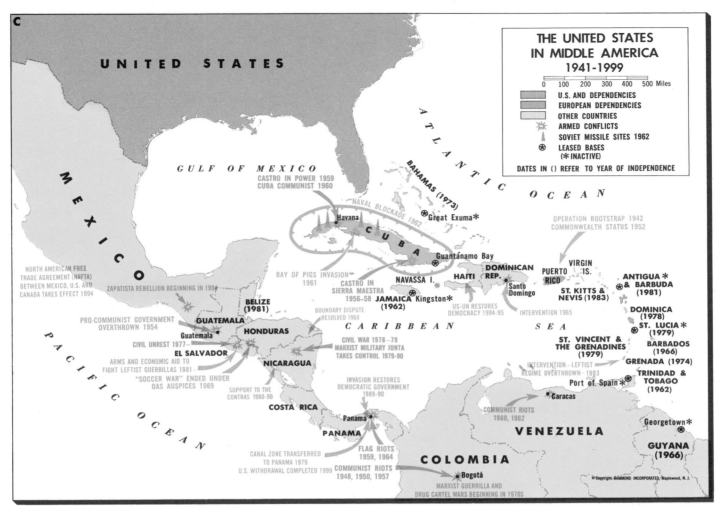

THE UNITED STATES IN MIDDLE AMERICA 1941-1999

0 100 200 300 400 500 Miles

U.S. AND DEPENDENCIES
EUROPEAN DEPENDENCIES
OTHER COUNTRIES
ARMED CONFLICTS
SOVIET MISSILE SITES 1962
LEASED BASES (*INACTIVE)

DATES IN ( ) REFER TO YEAR OF INDEPENDENCE

UNITED STATES

GULF OF MEXICO

MEXICO

ATLANTIC OCEAN

PACIFIC OCEAN

CASTRO IN POWER 1959
CUBA COMMUNIST 1960

BAHAMAS (1973)

NAVAL BLOCKADE 1962

Great Exuma*

Havana

CUBA

OPERATION BOOTSTRAP 1942
COMMONWEALTH STATUS 1952

NORTH AMERICAN FREE TRADE AGREEMENT (NAFTA) BETWEEN MEXICO, U.S. AND CANADA TAKES EFFECT 1994

ZAPATISTA REBELLION BEGINNING IN 1994

Guantánamo Bay

BAY OF PIGS INVASION 1961

CASTRO IN SIERRA MAESTRA 1956–58

NAVASSA I.

HAITI

DOMINICAN REP.

VIRGIN IS.

PUERTO RICO

ANTIGUA * & BARBUDA (1981)

Santo Domingo

ST. KITTS & NEVIS (1983)

DOMINICA (1978)

ST. LUCIA * (1979)

BELIZE (1981)

PRO-COMMUNIST GOVERNMENT OVERTHROWN 1954

GUATEMALA

Guatemala

HONDURAS

CIVIL UNREST 1977–

EL SALVADOR

ARMS AND ECONOMIC AID TO FIGHT LEFTIST GUERRILLAS 1981

"SOCCER WAR" ENDED UNDER OAS AUSPICES 1969

NICARAGUA

SUPPORT TO THE CONTRAS 1980–90

COSTA RICA

JAMAICA Kingston*
(1962)

BOUNDARY DISPUTE RESOLVED 1960

US-UN RESTORES DEMOCRACY 1994-95

INTERVENTION 1965

CARIBBEAN SEA

CIVIL WAR 1978–79 MARXIST MILITARY JUNTA TAKES CONTROL 1979-90

ST. VINCENT & THE GRENADINES (1979)

BARBADOS (1966)

GRENADA (1974)

INVASION RESTORES DEMOCRATIC GOVERNMENT 1989-90

Panama

PANAMA

CANAL ZONE TRANSFERRED TO PANAMA 1979

U.S. WITHDRAWAL COMPLETED 1999

FLAG RIOTS 1959, 1964

COMMUNIST RIOTS 1948, 1950, 1957

INTERVENTION—LEFTIST REGIME OVERTHROWN—1983

Port of Spain*

TRINIDAD & TOBAGO (1962)

COMMUNIST RIOTS 1960, 1962

Caracas

VENEZUELA

Georgetown*

GUYANA (1966)

COLOMBIA

Bogotá

MARXIST GUERRILLA AND DRUG CARTEL WARS BEGINNING IN 1970S

© Copyright HAMMOND INCORPORATED, Maplewood, N.J.

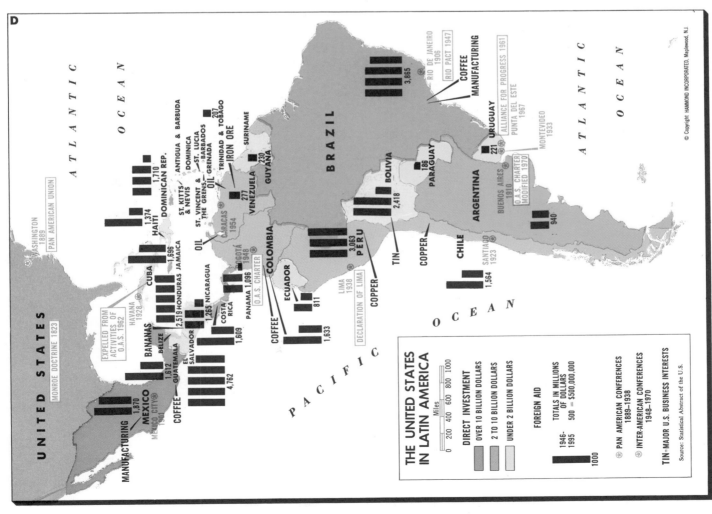

THE UNITED STATES IN LATIN AMERICA

Miles
0 200 400 600 800 1000

DIRECT INVESTMENT
OVER 10 BILLION DOLLARS
2 TO 10 BILLION DOLLARS
UNDER 2 BILLION DOLLARS

FOREIGN AID
TOTALS IN MILLIONS OF DOLLARS
500 = $500,000,000

1946–1995
1000

PAN AMERICAN CONFERENCES 1889–1938
INTER-AMERICAN CONFERENCES 1948–1970

TIN=MAJOR U.S. BUSINESS INTERESTS

Source: Statistical Abstract of the U.S.

UNITED STATES

ATLANTIC OCEAN

PACIFIC OCEAN

WASHINGTON 1889
PAN AMERICAN UNION

MONROE DOCTRINE 1823

MANUFACTURING

MEXICO 1,870
MEXICO CITY 1901

COFFEE

EXPELLED FROM ACTIVITIES OF O.A.S. 1962

HAVANA 1928

CUBA 1,710

BANANAS

BELIZE
GUATEMALA 1,612
EL SALVADOR

4,762

DOMINICAN REP.

HAITI 1,374

JAMAICA 1,696

HONDURAS 2,519

NICARAGUA 1,265

COSTA RICA 1,609

PANAMA 1,096
O.A.S. CHARTER 1948

ANTIGUA & BARBUDA
DOMINICA
ST. LUCIA
BARBADOS
GRENADA
ST. KITTS & NEVIS
ST. VINCENT & THE GRENS.
TRINIDAD & TOBAGO 207

IRON ORE

OIL

VENEZUELA 277
CARACAS 1954

230
GUYANA
SURINAME

COLOMBIA
BOGOTÁ 1948
O.A.S. CHARTER

ECUADOR 811

COFFEE 1,633

PERU 3,063
LIMA 1938
DECLARATION OF LIMA

COFFEE

COPPER

TIN

BRAZIL

3,865

COFFEE MANUFACTURING

RIO DE JANEIRO 1906
RIO PACT 1947

BOLIVIA

186 PARAGUAY
ASUNCIÓN

URUGUAY 221
MONTEVIDEO 1933

ALLIANCE FOR PROGRESS 1961
PUNTA DEL ESTE 1967

ARGENTINA
BUENOS AIRES 1910
O.A.S. CHARTER MODIFIED 1970

2,418

CHILE 1,564
SANTIAGO 1923

COPPER

940

ATLANTIC OCEAN

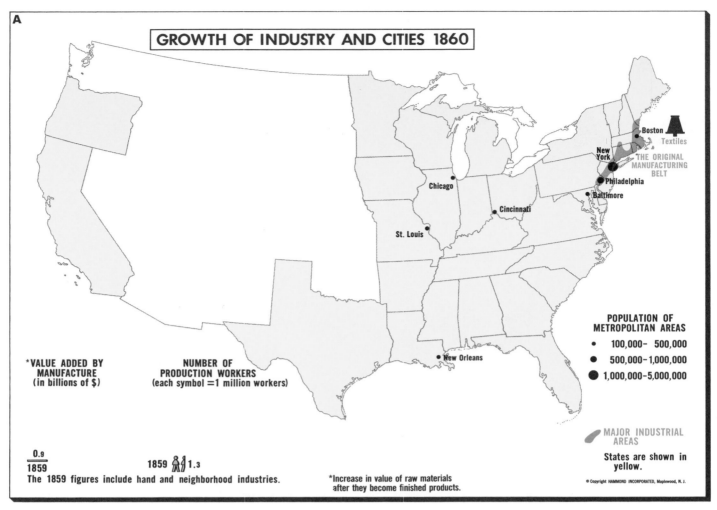

A

GROWTH OF INDUSTRY AND CITIES 1860

Boston

Textiles

New York

THE ORIGINAL MANUFACTURING BELT

Chicago

Philadelphia

Baltimore

Cincinnati

St. Louis

New Orleans

POPULATION OF METROPOLITAN AREAS

· 100,000- 500,000

● 500,000-1,000,000

⬤ 1,000,000-5,000,000

*VALUE ADDED BY MANUFACTURE (in billions of $)

NUMBER OF PRODUCTION WORKERS (each symbol =1 million workers)

MAJOR INDUSTRIAL AREAS

States are shown in yellow.

$\dfrac{0.9}{1859}$

1859 🧍1.3

The 1859 figures include hand and neighborhood industries.

*Increase in value of raw materials after they become finished products.

© Copyright HAMMOND INCORPORATED, Maplewood, N.J.

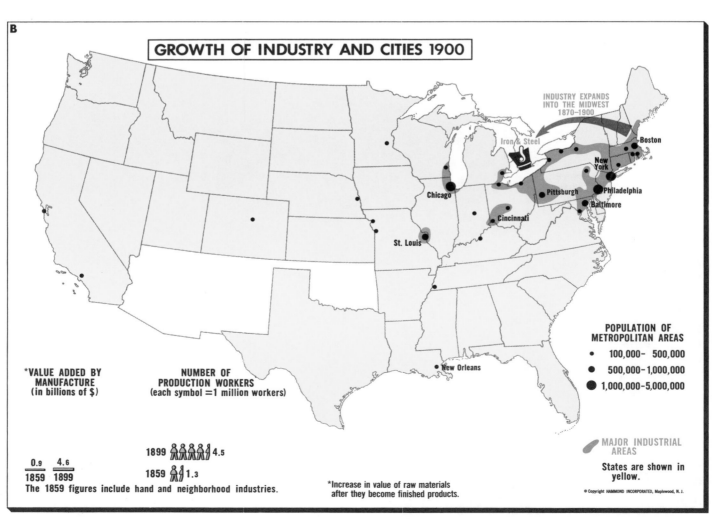

B

GROWTH OF INDUSTRY AND CITIES 1900

INDUSTRY EXPANDS INTO THE MIDWEST 1870–1900

Iron & Steel

Boston

New York

Chicago

Pittsburgh

Philadelphia

Baltimore

Cincinnati

St. Louis

New Orleans

POPULATION OF METROPOLITAN AREAS

· 100,000- 500,000

● 500,000-1,000,000

⬤ 1,000,000-5,000,000

*VALUE ADDED BY MANUFACTURE (in billions of $)

NUMBER OF PRODUCTION WORKERS (each symbol =1 million workers)

MAJOR INDUSTRIAL AREAS

States are shown in yellow.

1899 🧍🧍🧍🧍🧍4.5

$\dfrac{0.9}{1859} \quad \dfrac{4.6}{1899}$

1859 🧍1.3

The 1859 figures include hand and neighborhood industries.

*Increase in value of raw materials after they become finished products.

© Copyright HAMMOND INCORPORATED, Maplewood, N.J.

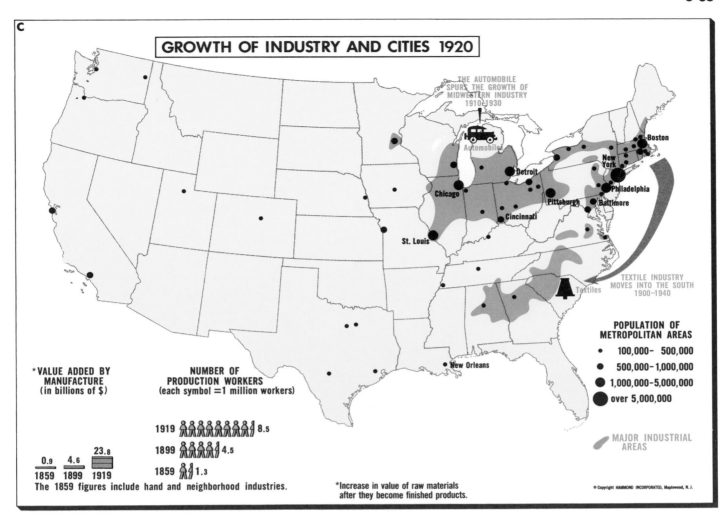

C

GROWTH OF INDUSTRY AND CITIES 1920

THE AUTOMOBILE SPURS THE GROWTH OF MIDWESTERN INDUSTRY 1910–1930

Automobiles

Boston
New York
Detroit
Philadelphia
Chicago
Pittsburgh
Baltimore
Cincinnati
St. Louis

Textiles

TEXTILE INDUSTRY MOVES INTO THE SOUTH 1900–1940

New Orleans

POPULATION OF METROPOLITAN AREAS
- · 100,000– 500,000
- • 500,000–1,000,000
- ● 1,000,000–5,000,000
- ⬤ over 5,000,000

MAJOR INDUSTRIAL AREAS

*VALUE ADDED BY MANUFACTURE (in billions of $)

NUMBER OF PRODUCTION WORKERS (each symbol = 1 million workers)

1919 8.5
1899 4.5
1859 1.3

0.9 — 1859
4.6 — 1899
23.8 — 1919

The 1859 figures include hand and neighborhood industries.

*Increase in value of raw materials after they become finished products.

© Copyright HAMMOND INCORPORATED, Maplewood, N.J.

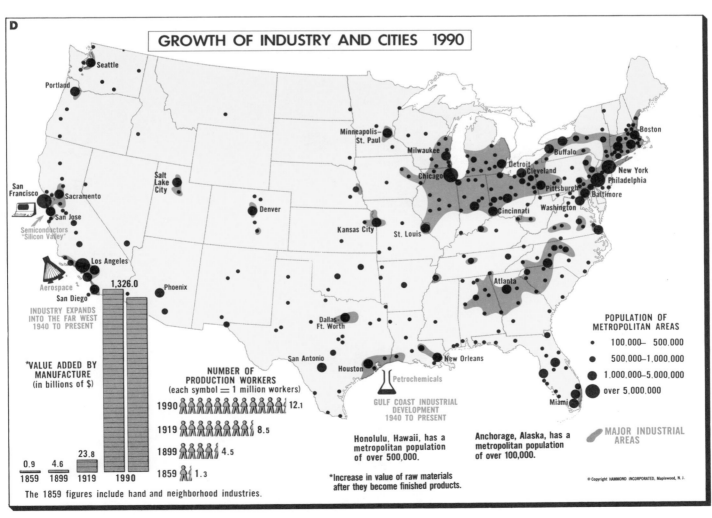

D

GROWTH OF INDUSTRY AND CITIES 1990

Seattle
Portland
Minneapolis St. Paul
Milwaukee
Buffalo
Boston
Detroit
Cleveland
New York
Salt Lake City
Chicago
Pittsburgh
Philadelphia
San Francisco
Sacramento
Denver
Cincinnati
Washington
Baltimore

Semiconductors "Silicon Valley"
San Jose

Kansas City
St. Louis

Los Angeles
Aerospace
San Diego
Phoenix
Atlanta

INDUSTRY EXPANDS INTO THE FAR WEST 1940 TO PRESENT

Dallas Ft. Worth

San Antonio
Houston
New Orleans
Miami

Petrochemicals

GULF COAST INDUSTRIAL DEVELOPMENT 1940 TO PRESENT

*VALUE ADDED BY MANUFACTURE (in billions of $)

1,326.0

NUMBER OF PRODUCTION WORKERS (each symbol = 1 million workers)

1990 12.1
1919 8.5
1899 4.5
1859 1.3

0.9 — 1859
4.6 — 1899
23.8 — 1919
1,326.0 — 1990

The 1859 figures include hand and neighborhood industries.

Honolulu, Hawaii, has a metropolitan population of over 500,000.

Anchorage, Alaska, has a metropolitan population of over 100,000.

*Increase in value of raw materials after they become finished products.

POPULATION OF METROPOLITAN AREAS
- · 100,000– 500,000
- • 500,000–1,000,000
- ● 1,000,000–5,000,000
- ⬤ over 5,000,000

MAJOR INDUSTRIAL AREAS

© Copyright HAMMOND INCORPORATED, Maplewood, N.J.

A

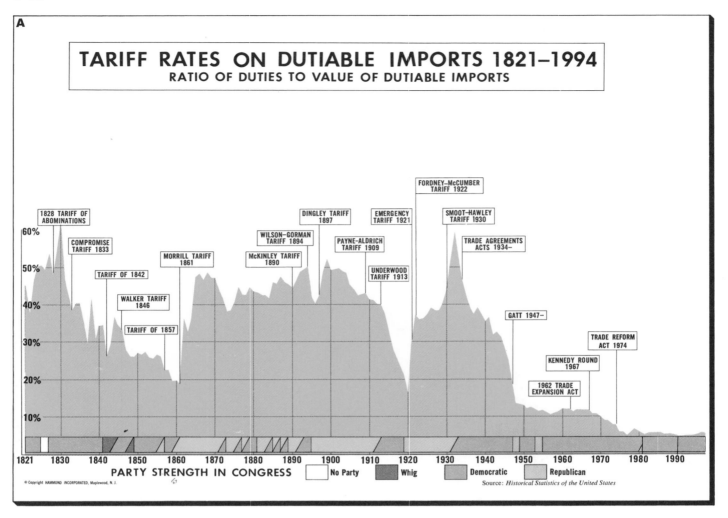

TARIFF RATES ON DUTIABLE IMPORTS 1821–1994
RATIO OF DUTIES TO VALUE OF DUTIABLE IMPORTS

1828 TARIFF OF ABOMINATIONS

COMPROMISE TARIFF 1833

TARIFF OF 1842

WALKER TARIFF 1846

TARIFF OF 1857

MORRILL TARIFF 1861

McKINLEY TARIFF 1890

WILSON–GORMAN TARIFF 1894

DINGLEY TARIFF 1897

PAYNE–ALDRICH TARIFF 1909

EMERGENCY TARIFF 1921

UNDERWOOD TARIFF 1913

FORDNEY–McCUMBER TARIFF 1922

SMOOT–HAWLEY TARIFF 1930

TRADE AGREEMENTS ACTS 1934–

GATT 1947–

KENNEDY ROUND 1967

1962 TRADE EXPANSION ACT

TRADE REFORM ACT 1974

60%
50%
40%
30%
20%
10%

1821 1830 1840 1850 1860 1870 1880 1890 1900 1910 1920 1930 1940 1950 1960 1970 1980 1990

PARTY STRENGTH IN CONGRESS

No Party | Whig | Democratic | Republican

© Copyright HAMMOND INCORPORATED, Maplewood, N.J.

Source: *Historical Statistics of the United States*

B

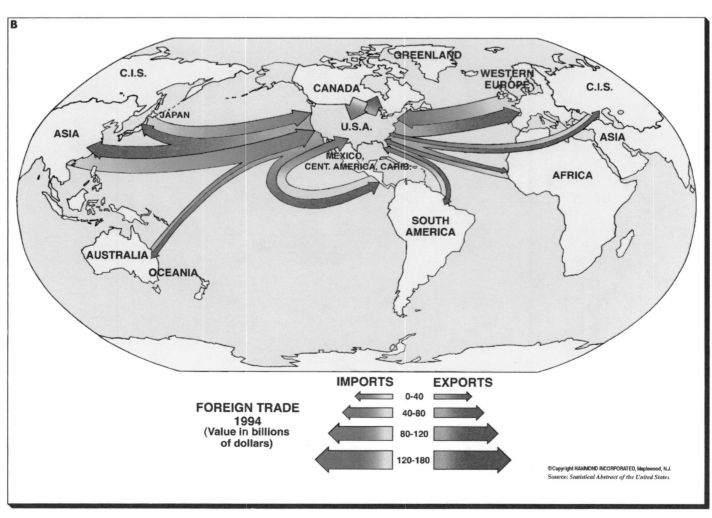

GREENLAND

C.I.S.

CANADA

WESTERN EUROPE

C.I.S.

JAPAN

ASIA

U.S.A.

ASIA

MEXICO, CENT. AMERICA, CARIB.

AFRICA

SOUTH AMERICA

AUSTRALIA

OCEANIA

IMPORTS   EXPORTS

FOREIGN TRADE 1994
(Value in billions of dollars)

0–40
40–80
80–120
120–180

©Copyright HAMMOND INCORPORATED, N.J.

Source: *Statistical Abstract of the United States*

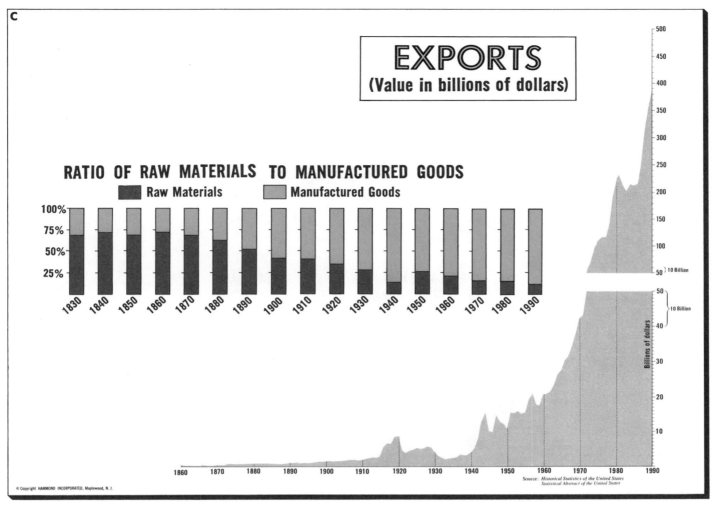

EXPORTS
(Value in billions of dollars)

RATIO OF RAW MATERIALS TO MANUFACTURED GOODS
- Raw Materials
- Manufactured Goods

Source: *Historical Statistics of the United States*
Statistical Abstract of the United States

© Copyright HAMMOND INCORPORATED, Maplewood, N. J.

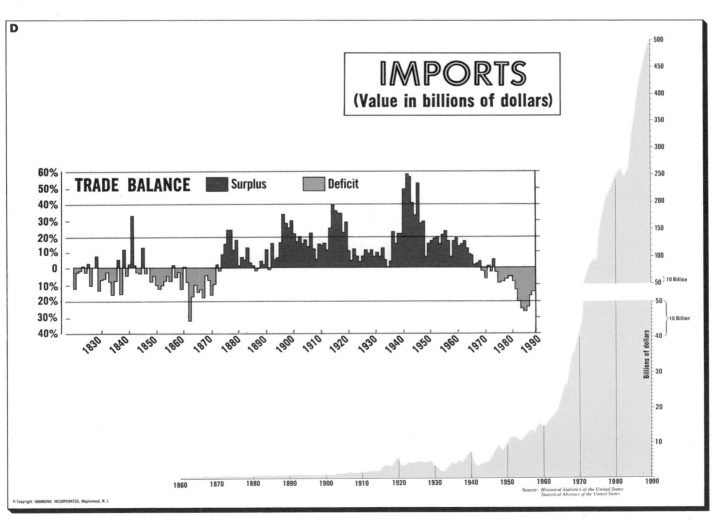

IMPORTS
(Value in billions of dollars)

TRADE BALANCE
- Surplus
- Deficit

Source: *Historical Statistics of the United States*
Statistical Abstract of the United States

© Copyright HAMMOND INCORPORATED, Maplewood, N. J.

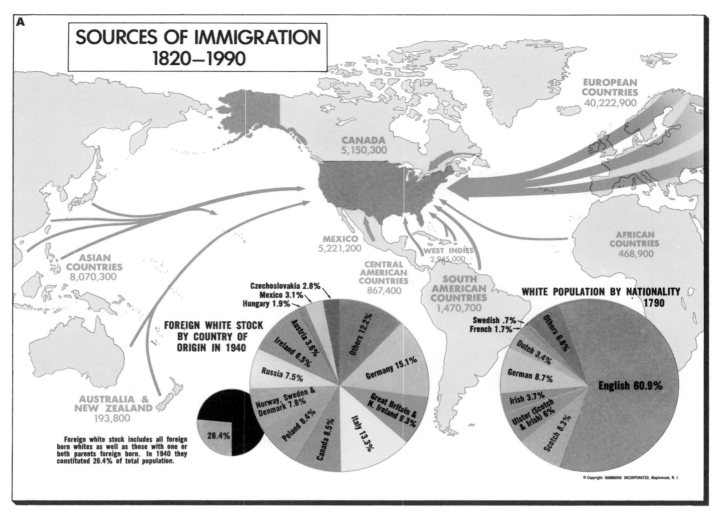

A

SOURCES OF IMMIGRATION
1820–1990

EUROPEAN COUNTRIES 40,222,900

CANADA 5,150,300

ASIAN COUNTRIES 8,070,300

MEXICO 5,221,200

WEST INDIES 2,945,000

CENTRAL AMERICAN COUNTRIES 867,400

SOUTH AMERICAN COUNTRIES 1,470,700

AFRICAN COUNTRIES 468,900

AUSTRALIA & NEW ZEALAND 193,800

FOREIGN WHITE STOCK BY COUNTRY OF ORIGIN IN 1940

Czechoslovakia 2.8%
Mexico 3.1%
Hungary 1.9%
Austria 3.6%
Ireland 6.5%
Russia 7.5%
Norway, Sweden & Denmark 7.8%
Poland 8.4%
Canada 8.5%
Italy 13.3%
Great Britain & N. Ireland 9.3%
Germany 15.1%
Others 12.2%

26.4%

Foreign white stock includes all foreign born whites as well as those with one or both parents foreign born. In 1940 they constituted 26.4% of total population.

WHITE POPULATION BY NATIONALITY 1790

Swedish .7%
French 1.7%
Others 6.6%
Dutch 3.4%
German 8.7%
Irish 3.7%
Ulster (Scotch & Irish) 6%
Scotch 8.3%
English 60.9%

© Copyright HAMMOND INCORPORATED, Maplewood, N. J.

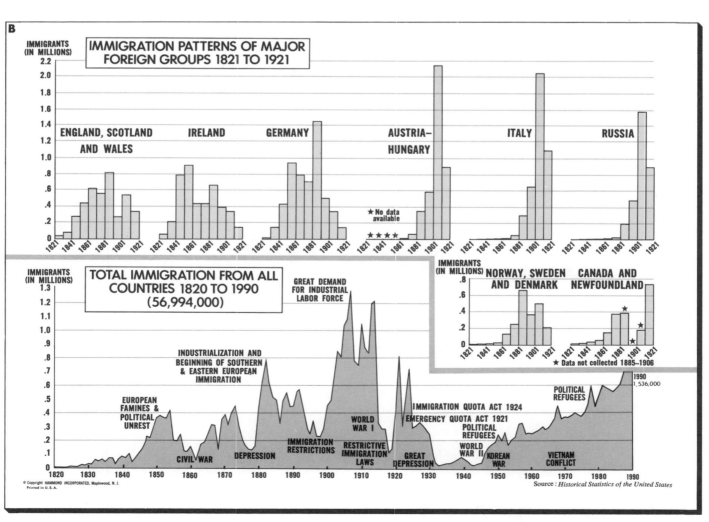

B

IMMIGRATION PATTERNS OF MAJOR FOREIGN GROUPS 1821 TO 1921

IMMIGRANTS (IN MILLIONS)

ENGLAND, SCOTLAND AND WALES

IRELAND

GERMANY

AUSTRIA–HUNGARY

★ No data available

ITALY

RUSSIA

TOTAL IMMIGRATION FROM ALL COUNTRIES 1820 TO 1990 (56,994,000)

IMMIGRANTS (IN MILLIONS)

GREAT DEMAND FOR INDUSTRIAL LABOR FORCE

INDUSTRIALIZATION AND BEGINNING OF SOUTHERN & EASTERN EUROPEAN IMMIGRATION

EUROPEAN FAMINES & POLITICAL UNREST

CIVIL WAR

DEPRESSION

IMMIGRATION RESTRICTIONS

WORLD WAR I

RESTRICTIVE IMMIGRATION LAWS

IMMIGRATION QUOTA ACT 1924

EMERGENCY QUOTA ACT 1921 POLITICAL REFUGEES

GREAT DEPRESSION

WORLD WAR II

KOREAN WAR

POLITICAL REFUGEES

VIETNAM CONFLICT

1990 1,536,000

IMMIGRANTS (IN MILLIONS)

NORWAY, SWEDEN AND DENMARK

CANADA AND NEWFOUNDLAND

★ Data not collected 1885–1906

© Copyright HAMMOND INCORPORATED, Maplewood, N. J.
Printed in U. S. A.

Source : *Historical Statistics of the United States*

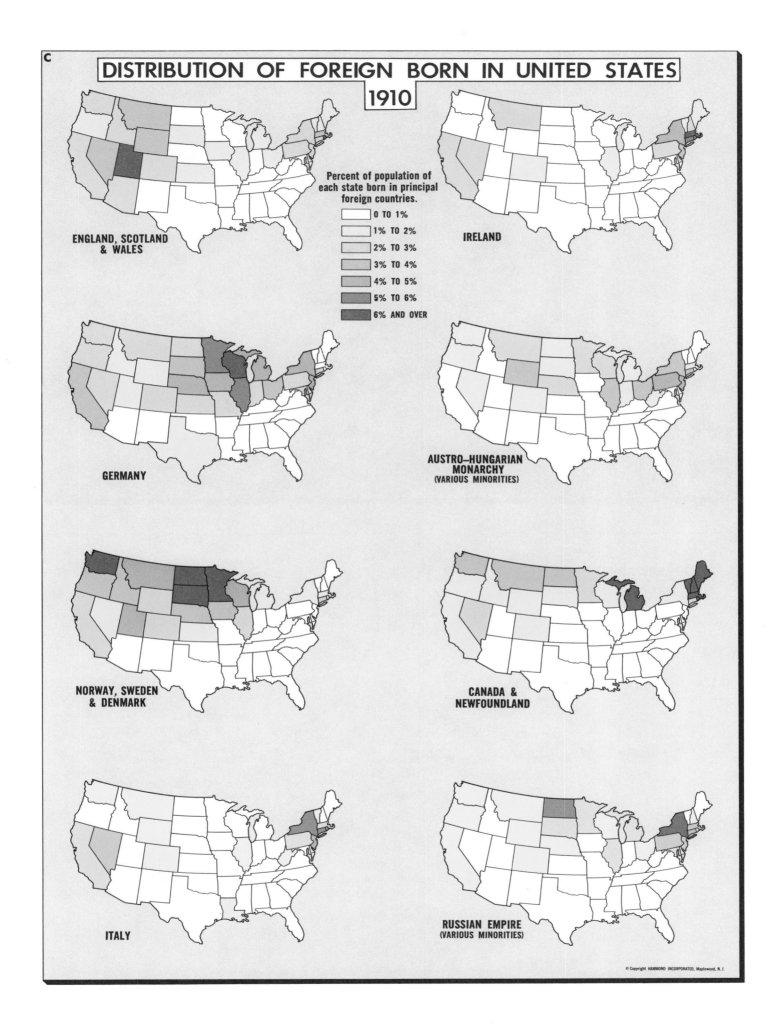

DISTRIBUTION OF FOREIGN BORN IN UNITED STATES
1910

Percent of population of each state born in principal foreign countries.

- 0 TO 1%
- 1% TO 2%
- 2% TO 3%
- 3% TO 4%
- 4% TO 5%
- 5% TO 6%
- 6% AND OVER

ENGLAND, SCOTLAND & WALES

IRELAND

GERMANY

AUSTRO—HUNGARIAN MONARCHY (VARIOUS MINORITIES)

NORWAY, SWEDEN & DENMARK

CANADA & NEWFOUNDLAND

ITALY

RUSSIAN EMPIRE (VARIOUS MINORITIES)

© Copyright HAMMOND INCORPORATED, Maplewood, N. J.

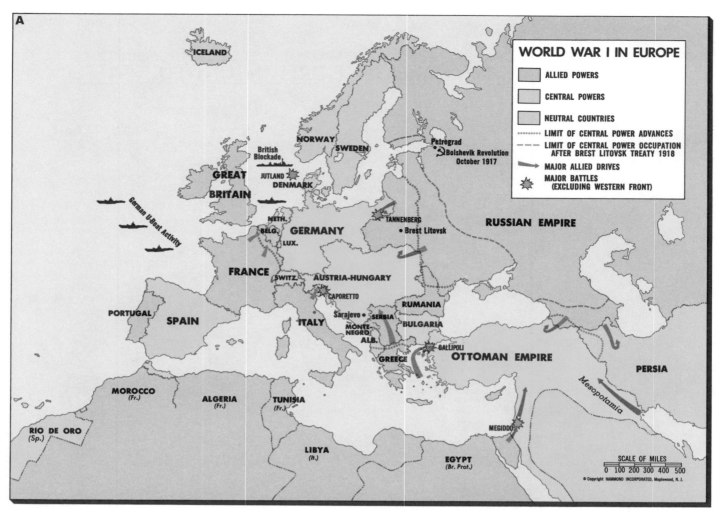

A

WORLD WAR I IN EUROPE

- ALLIED POWERS
- CENTRAL POWERS
- NEUTRAL COUNTRIES
- ···· LIMIT OF CENTRAL POWER ADVANCES
- --- LIMIT OF CENTRAL POWER OCCUPATION AFTER BREST LITOVSK TREATY 1918
- ➤ MAJOR ALLIED DRIVES
- ✸ MAJOR BATTLES (EXCLUDING WESTERN FRONT)

ICELAND

NORWAY
SWEDEN
GREAT BRITAIN
British Blockade
JUTLAND
DENMARK
NETH.
BELG.
GERMANY
LUX.
German U-Boat Activity
Petrograd
Bolshevik Revolution October 1917
TANNENBERG
Brest Litovsk
RUSSIAN EMPIRE
FRANCE
SWITZ.
AUSTRIA-HUNGARY
CAPORETTO
PORTUGAL
SPAIN
ITALY
Sarajevo
SERBIA
MONTE-NEGRO
ALB.
RUMANIA
BULGARIA
GREECE
GALLIPOLI
OTTOMAN EMPIRE
PERSIA
Mesopotamia
MOROCCO (Fr.)
ALGERIA (Fr.)
TUNISIA (Fr.)
MEGIDDO
RIO DE ORO (Sp.)
LIBYA (It.)
EGYPT (Br. Prot.)

SCALE OF MILES
0 100 200 300 400 500
© Copyright HAMMOND INCORPORATED, Maplewood, N.J.

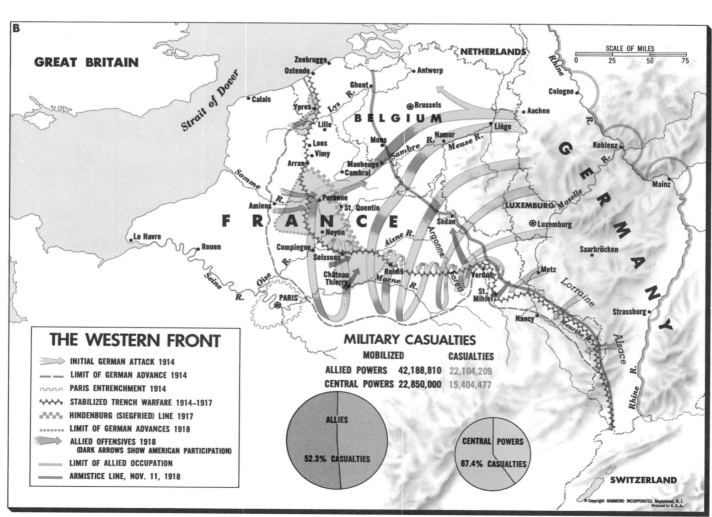

B

GREAT BRITAIN

NETHERLANDS
Rhine R.

Strait of Dover
Calais
Zeebrugge
Ostende
Ghent
Antwerp
Ypres
Lys R.
Lille
Loos
Vimy
Arras
BELGIUM
Brussels
Mons
Namur
Meuse R.
Liège
Aachen
Cologne
Koblenz
Sambre R.
Maubeuge
Cambrai
Somme R.
Peronne
St. Quentin
Amiens
FRANCE
Noyon
Compiegne
Oise R.
Soissons
Aisne R.
Sedan
LUXEMBURG
Moselle R.
Luxemburg
Mainz
GERMANY
Le Havre
Rouen
Seine R.
Château Thierry
Reims
Marne R.
Argonne Forest
Verdun
St. Mihiel
Metz
Saarbrücken
PARIS
Nancy
Lorraine
Strassburg
Meurthe R.
Alsace
Rhine R.
SWITZERLAND

SCALE OF MILES
0 25 50 75

THE WESTERN FRONT

- ➤ INITIAL GERMAN ATTACK 1914
- --- LIMIT OF GERMAN ADVANCE 1914
- ∿∿∿ PARIS ENTRENCHMENT 1914
- ✕✕✕ STABILIZED TRENCH WARFARE 1914–1917
- ▨▨▨ HINDENBURG (SIEGFRIED) LINE 1917
- ···· LIMIT OF GERMAN ADVANCES 1918
- ➤ ALLIED OFFENSIVES 1918 (DARK ARROWS SHOW AMERICAN PARTICIPATION)
- — LIMIT OF ALLIED OCCUPATION
- — ARMISTICE LINE, NOV. 11, 1918

MILITARY CASUALTIES

	MOBILIZED	CASUALTIES
ALLIED POWERS	42,188,810	22,104,209
CENTRAL POWERS	22,850,000	15,404,477

ALLIES
52.3% CASUALTIES

CENTRAL POWERS
67.4% CASUALTIES

© Copyright HAMMOND INCORPORATED, Maplewood, N.J.
Printed in U.S.A.

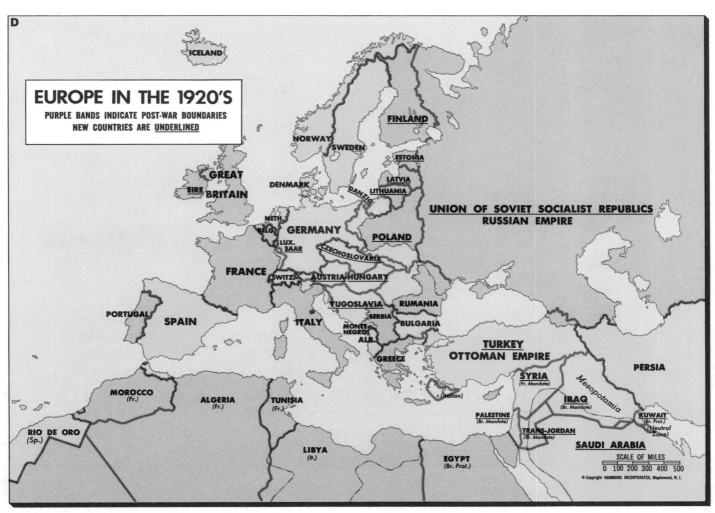

C

AISNE-MARNE OFFENSIVE
July 18–August 6, 1918

0   5   10   15   20 MILES

Oise R.
Aisne R.
Soissons
FRENCH TENTH ARMY
Buzancy
July 20
Forest of Villers-Cotterêts
July 28
Aug. 6 Vesle R.
Fismes
18
U.S. III CORPS
July 28
Rheims
Ourcq R.
July 20
F R A N C E
Sergy
July 20
FRENCH FIFTH ARMY
FRENCH SIXTH ARMY
July 18
Dormans
Belleau Wood
June 6–July 10, 1918
Château-Thierry
July 18
Épernay
Marne R.
Marne R.
FRENCH NINTH ARMY

ST. MIHIEL OFFENSIVE
September 12–16, 1918

0   5   10 MILES

Étain
Verdun
Haudimont
Mars-la-Tour
Metz
Moselle R.
Meuse R.
U.S. V CORPS
Sept. 16
Chambley
F R A N C E
GERMANY
Troyon
Hattonchâtel
Thiaucourt
Selle R.
U.S. FIRST ARMY
Sept. 12
St. Mihiel
Apremont
Sept. 12
Pont-à-Mousson
U.S. IV CORPS
U.S. I CORPS
FRENCH II COLONIAL CORPS

Meuse R.
Sedan
Chiers R.
BELGIUM
LUXEMBURG
Mouzon
Ardennes R.
Beaumont
Le Chesne
Stenay
Nov. 11
Nov. 3
Chiers R.
Moselle R.
F R A N C E
Jametz
Loison R.
Thionville
Buzancy
Meuse R.
Dun-sur-Meuse
Damvillers
Grandpré
Romagne
Brieulles
Côtes de Meuse
Nov. 1
Nov. 1
Orne R.
Apremont
Montfaucon
Sept. 26
Nov. 11
Étain
GERMANY
Argonne Forest
Varennes
Sept. 26
Metz
Aisne R.
Aire R.
Verdun
Riaville
FRENCH FOURTH ARMY
Ste. Menehould
U.S. FIRST ARMY
Meuse R.
Sept. 26
Meuse R.

MEUSE – ARGONNE OFFENSIVE
September 26–November 11, 1918

0   5   10   15   20 MILES

Haumont-les-Lachaussée
Nov. 11
U.S. SECOND ARMY
Pont-à-Mousson

THE WESTERN FRONT 1918
REDUCTION OF THE SALIENTS AND FINAL OFFENSIVE

➡ ALLIED OFFENSIVES (DARK ARROWS SHOW AMERICAN PARTICIPATION)

┄┄ } FRONT LINES

━━ ARMISTICE LINE, NOVEMBER 11, 1918

© Copyright HAMMOND INCORPORATED, Maplewood, N. J.

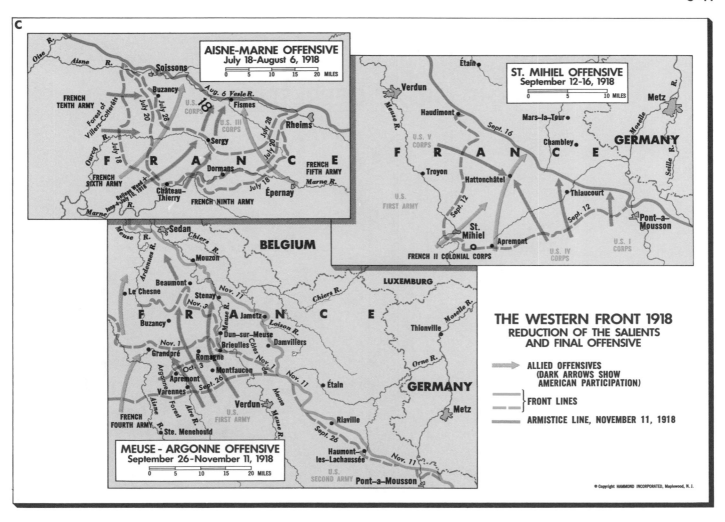

D

EUROPE IN THE 1920'S
PURPLE BANDS INDICATE POST-WAR BOUNDARIES
NEW COUNTRIES ARE <u>UNDERLINED</u>

ICELAND
FINLAND
NORWAY
SWEDEN
ESTONIA
GREAT BRITAIN
EIRE
DENMARK
LATVIA
DANZIG
LITHUANIA
UNION OF SOVIET SOCIALIST REPUBLICS
RUSSIAN EMPIRE
NETH.
BELG.
GERMANY
POLAND
LUX.
SAAR
CZECHOSLOVAKIA
FRANCE
SWITZ.
AUSTRIA-HUNGARY
PORTUGAL
SPAIN
ITALY
YUGOSLAVIA
SERBIA
RUMANIA
MONTE-NEGRO
ALB.
BULGARIA
GREECE
(Italian)
TURKEY
OTTOMAN EMPIRE
PERSIA
SYRIA (Fr. Mandate)
Mesopotamia
MOROCCO (Fr.)
ALGERIA (Fr.)
TUNISIA (Fr.)
IRAQ (Br. Mandate)
KUWAIT (Br. Prot.) (Neutral Zone)
PALESTINE (Br. Mandate)
RIO DE ORO (Sp.)
LIBYA (It.)
TRANS-JORDAN (Br. Mandate)
SAUDI ARABIA
EGYPT (Br. Prot.)

SCALE OF MILES
0 100 200 300 400 500

© Copyright HAMMOND INCORPORATED, Maplewood, N. J.

THE GREAT DEPRESSION

A

THE DECLINE AND RECOVERY OF THE NATIONAL ECONOMY

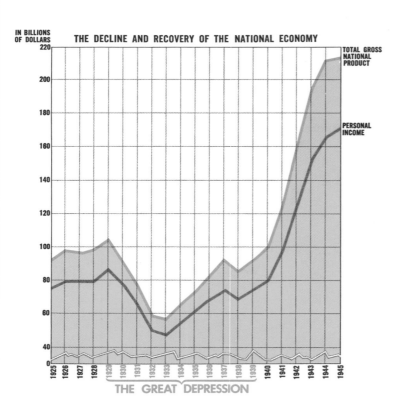

IN BILLIONS OF DOLLARS

TOTAL GROSS NATIONAL PRODUCT

PERSONAL INCOME

THE GREAT DEPRESSION

NUMBER OF BANK SUSPENSIONS 1919–1933

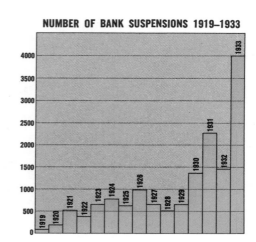

UNEMPLOYMENT

THE UNEMPLOYED AS A PERCENT OF THE CIVILIAN LABOR FORCE

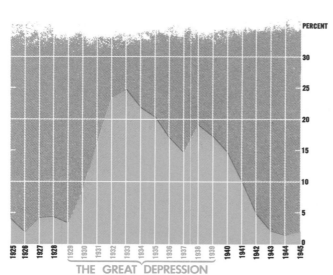

THE GREAT DEPRESSION

HOW U.S. TOTAL PERSONAL INCOME WAS DIVIDED IN 1929

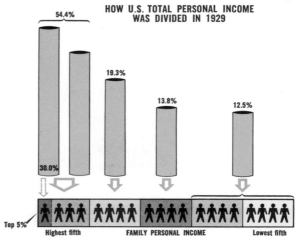

54.4%

19.3%

13.8%

12.5%

30.0%

Top 5%

Highest fifth   FAMILY PERSONAL INCOME   Lowest fifth

HOURS WORKED IN MANUFACTURING (1925–1945) (WEEKLY AVERAGE)

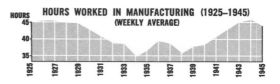

HOURS

© Copyright HAMMOND INCORPORATED, Maplewood, N.J.

Source: *Historical Statistics of the United States*

B

THE GREAT DEPRESSION
SPECULATION IN THE STOCK MARKET

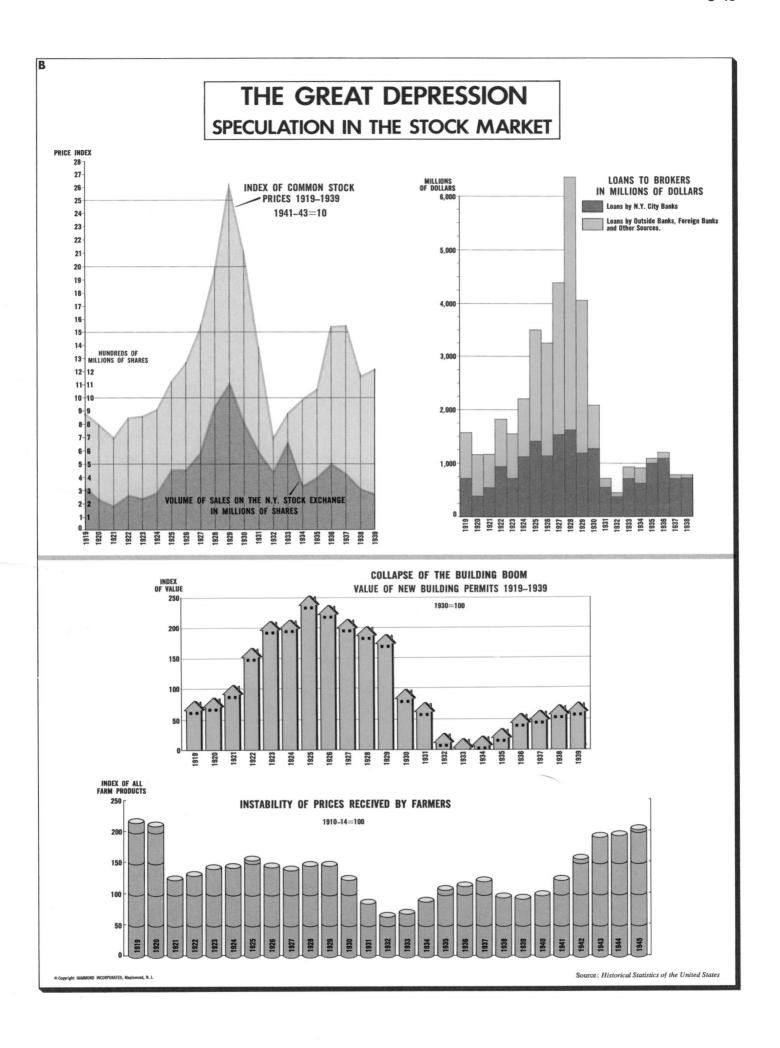

PRICE INDEX

INDEX OF COMMON STOCK PRICES 1919–1939
1941–43=10

HUNDREDS OF MILLIONS OF SHARES

VOLUME OF SALES ON THE N.Y. STOCK EXCHANGE IN MILLIONS OF SHARES

MILLIONS OF DOLLARS

LOANS TO BROKERS IN MILLIONS OF DOLLARS
- Loans by N.Y. City Banks
- Loans by Outside Banks, Foreign Banks and Other Sources.

COLLAPSE OF THE BUILDING BOOM
VALUE OF NEW BUILDING PERMITS 1919–1939

INDEX OF VALUE

1930=100

INDEX OF ALL FARM PRODUCTS

INSTABILITY OF PRICES RECEIVED BY FARMERS

1910–14=100

© Copyright HAMMOND INCORPORATED, Maplewood, N.J.

Source: *Historical Statistics of the United States*

A

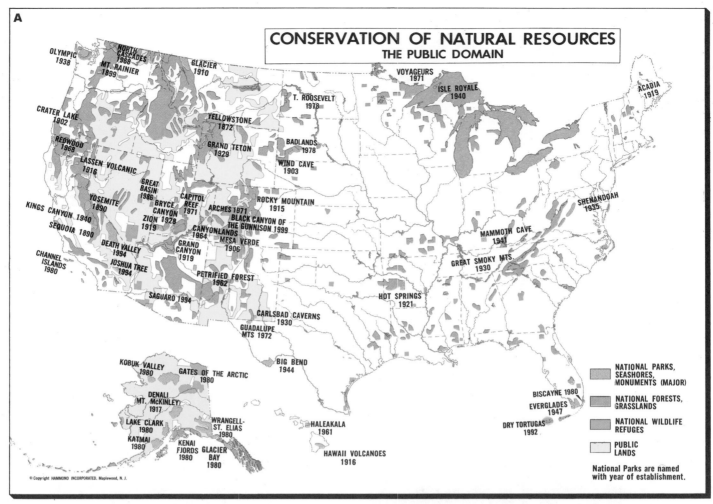

CONSERVATION OF NATURAL RESOURCES
THE PUBLIC DOMAIN

National Parks, Seashores, Monuments (Major)

National Forests, Grasslands

National Wildlife Refuges

Public Lands

National Parks are named with year of establishment.

B

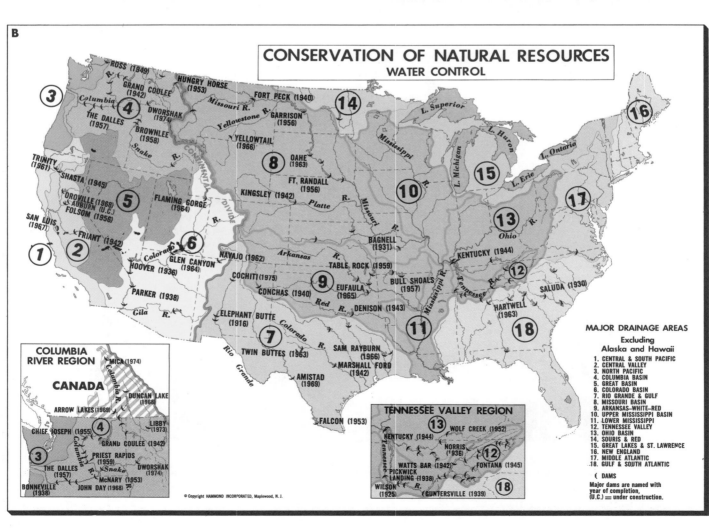

CONSERVATION OF NATURAL RESOURCES
WATER CONTROL

MAJOR DRAINAGE AREAS
Excluding Alaska and Hawaii

1. CENTRAL & SOUTH PACIFIC
2. CENTRAL VALLEY
3. NORTH PACIFIC
4. COLUMBIA BASIN
5. GREAT BASIN
6. COLORADO BASIN
7. RIO GRANDE & GULF
8. MISSOURI BASIN
9. ARKANSAS—WHITE—RED
10. UPPER MISSISSIPPI BASIN
11. LOWER MISSISSIPPI
12. TENNESSEE VALLEY
13. OHIO BASIN
14. SOURIS & RED
15. GREAT LAKES & ST. LAWRENCE
16. NEW ENGLAND
17. MIDDLE ATLANTIC
18. GULF & SOUTH ATLANTIC

⟨ DAMS

Major dams are named with year of completion,
(U.C.) = under construction.

© Copyright HAMMOND INCORPORATED, Maplewood, N. J.

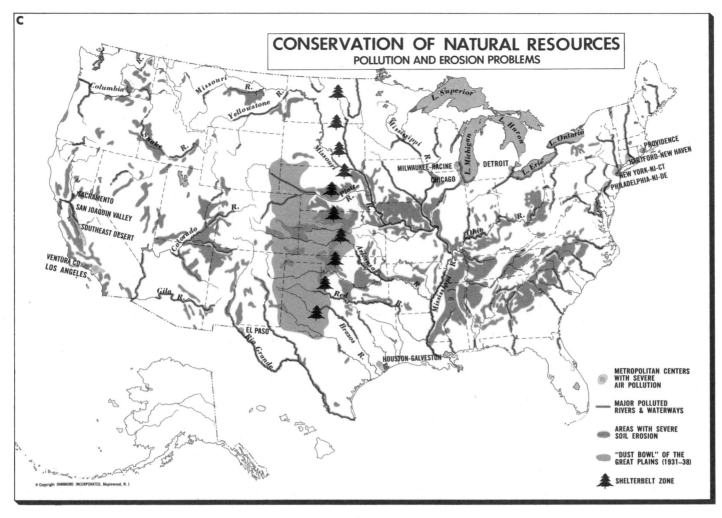

C

CONSERVATION OF NATURAL RESOURCES
POLLUTION AND EROSION PROBLEMS

- ○ METROPOLITAN CENTERS WITH SEVERE AIR POLLUTION
- — MAJOR POLLUTED RIVERS & WATERWAYS
- ◉ AREAS WITH SEVERE SOIL EROSION
- ◉ "DUST BOWL" OF THE GREAT PLAINS (1931–38)
- 🌲 SHELTERBELT ZONE

© Copyright HAMMOND INCORPORATED, Maplewood, N.J.

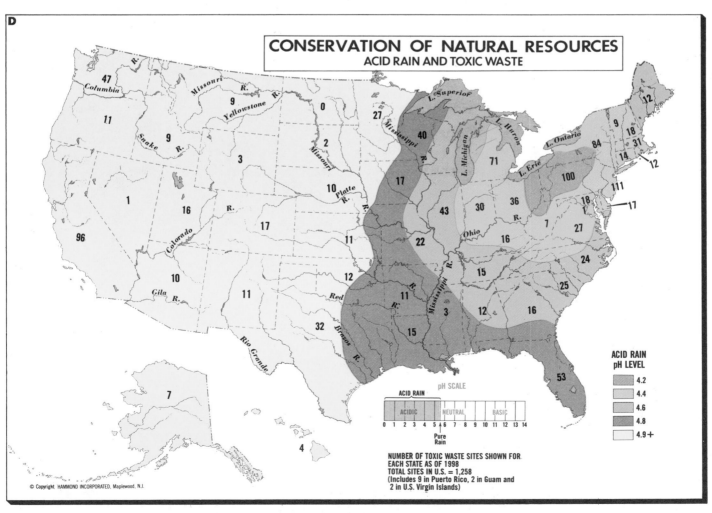

D

CONSERVATION OF NATURAL RESOURCES
ACID RAIN AND TOXIC WASTE

ACID RAIN pH LEVEL
- 4.2
- 4.4
- 4.6
- 4.8
- 4.9+

pH SCALE
ACID RAIN | ACIDIC | NEUTRAL | BASIC
0 1 2 3 4 5 6 7 8 9 10 11 12 13 14
Pure Rain

NUMBER OF TOXIC WASTE SITES SHOWN FOR EACH STATE AS OF 1998
TOTAL SITES IN U.S. = 1,258
(Includes 9 in Puerto Rico, 2 in Guam and 2 in U.S. Virgin Islands)

© Copyright HAMMOND INCORPORATED, Maplewood, N.J.

A

GERMAN EXPANSION 1935-1939*

SCALE OF MILES

0 100 200 300 400

- Germany 1933
- Area gained by Plebiscite 1935
- Areas annexed 1938
- Area annexed 1939
- German Protectorates

*To Invasion of Poland Sept. 1, 1939

MEMEL To Germany 1939

Rhineland remilitarized 1936

BOHEMIA & MORAVIA German Protectorate and occupation 1939

SAAR To Germany 1935

SUDETENLAND To Germany 1938

To Hung. 1939

SLOVAKIA German Protectorate 1939

AUSTRIA To Germany 1938

Civil War 1936-1939

ALBANIA (To Italy 1939)

© Copyright HAMMOND INCORPORATED, Maplewood, N.J.

B

WORLD WAR II 1939-1940*

SCALE OF MILES

0 100 200 300 400

- Germany and Slovakia
- Allied Nations
- Neutral Nations
- Areas occupied by Germany
- Areas occupied by U.S.S.R.
- German Advances
- British Advances
- Russian Advances

*To July 1, 1940

International Boundaries Sept. 1, 1939

RUSSO–FINNISH WAR 1939-1940

German invasion of Norway and Denmark April 9, 1940

German invasion of Low Countries May 10, 1940

Estonia, Latvia and Lithuania annexed by U.S.S.R. 1940

Battle of France May–June 1940

German invasion of Poland September 1, 1939 Start of World War II

U.S.S.R. invasion of Poland September 17, 1939

Vichy Government established July 1940

Partition of Poland September 27, 1939

Bessarabia and northern Bukovina annexed by U.S.S.R. 1940

Italy declares war on Great Britain and France June 1940

© Copyright HAMMOND INCORPORATED, Maplewood, N.J.

C

WORLD WAR II EUROPEAN THEATER 1940-1942

- Allied Nations and Allied controlled Nations
- Axis Powers and Axis controlled Nations
- Neutral Nations
- Vichy France; Vichy controlled Areas (later to Allies)
- Areas occupied by Axis

German Air Strikes
Famous Battles or Sieges
German Advances
Allied Advances
Western Front
Eastern Front

ICELAND
British occupation 1940 U.S. occupation 1941 Independent 1944

SUPPLY ROUTE FROM U.S. & BRITISH COMMONWEALTH

NORWEGIAN SEA
Murmansk

NORTH SEA

SWEDEN
NORWAY
FINLAND
1941

UNITED KINGDOM
IRELAND
DENMARK
EST.
LATVIA
LITH.
Leningrad
1941
Moscow
1941

London
NETH.
BELG.
LUX.
Berlin
GERMANY
POLAND
1941
Ukraine
1941
1942
Stalingrad

UNION OF SOVIET SOCIALIST REPUBLICS

SUPPLY ROUTE FROM U.S.

German U-boat Blockade

Paris
VICHY FRANCE
SWITZ.
Austria
HUNGARY
1941
SLOVAKIA
RUMANIA

ATLANTIC OCEAN

PORTUGAL
SPAIN
Corsica
ITALY
Rome
Sardinia
YUGOSLAVIA
BULGARIA
ALB. (It.)
GREECE
1941

BLACK SEA

CASPIAN SEA

Axis influence removed after British and Russian invasion 1941

ALLIED SUPPLY ROUTE
IRAN

Gibraltar (Br.)
MEDITERRANEAN
TURKEY
Neutral until Feb. 1945
IRAN

SP. MOR.
Casablanca
Oran
Algiers
Tunis
Malta (Br.)
Sicily
Crete
Cyprus (Br.)
SYRIA (Fr.)
IRAQ

Canary Is. (Sp.)
MOROCCO (Fr.)
ALGERIA (Fr.)
TUNISIA (Fr.)
Tripoli
SEA
El Alamein
PALESTINE (Br. Mandate)
TRANS-JORDAN (Br. Mandate)

Pro-Axis government removed by British 1941
Persian Gulf

RIO DE ORO (Sp.)
LIBYA (It.)
1941
1942
1940
1942
Cairo
EGYPT
SAUDI ARABIA
Neutral until Mar. 1945

SCALE OF MILES
0 100 200 300 400 500
© Copyright HAMMOND INCORPORATED, Maplewood, N.J.

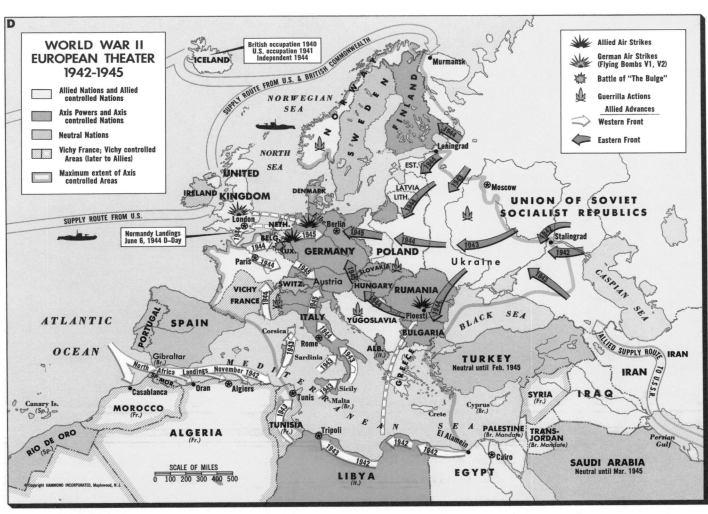

D

WORLD WAR II EUROPEAN THEATER 1942-1945

- Allied Nations and Allied controlled Nations
- Axis Powers and Axis controlled Nations
- Neutral Nations
- Vichy France; Vichy controlled Areas (later to Allies)
- Maximum extent of Axis controlled Areas

Allied Air Strikes
German Air Strikes (Flying Bombs V1, V2)
Battle of "The Bulge"
Guerrilla Actions
Allied Advances
Western Front
Eastern Front

ICELAND
British occupation 1940 U.S. occupation 1941 Independent 1944

SUPPLY ROUTE FROM U.S. & BRITISH COMMONWEALTH

NORWEGIAN SEA
Murmansk

NORWAY

NORTH SEA

SWEDEN
FINLAND
1944
Leningrad

UNITED KINGDOM
IRELAND
DENMARK
EST.
1944
1943
Moscow

LATVIA
LITH.

UNION OF SOVIET SOCIALIST REPUBLICS

SUPPLY ROUTE FROM U.S.

London
Normandy Landings June 6, 1944 D-Day
NETH.
BELG.
LUX.
1944
Berlin
1945
GERMANY
POLAND
1944
1943
Stalingrad
1942

Paris
1944
1945
VICHY FRANCE
1944
SWITZ.
Austria
SLOVAKIA
HUNGARY
1944
RUMANIA
Ukraine
1943
1944

ATLANTIC OCEAN

PORTUGAL
SPAIN
Corsica
1943
Rome
1944
ITALY
Sardinia
1943
YUGOSLAVIA
Ploesti
1944
BULGARIA
ALB. (It.)
GREECE

BLACK SEA

CASPIAN SEA

Gibraltar (Br.)
North Africa Landings November 1942
MEDITERRANEAN
1945
TURKEY
Neutral until Feb. 1945
ALLIED SUPPLY ROUTE
IRAN
IRAN

SP. MOR.
Casablanca
Oran
Algiers
1943
Tunis
Malta (Br.)
Sicily
Crete
Cyprus (Br.)
SYRIA (Fr.)
IRAQ

Canary Is. (Sp.)
MOROCCO (Fr.)
ALGERIA (Fr.)
TUNISIA (Fr.)
1943
Tripoli
1942
SEA
El Alamein
1942
PALESTINE (Br. Mandate)
TRANS-JORDAN (Br. Mandate)

Persian Gulf

RIO DE ORO (Sp.)
LIBYA (It.)
1942
Cairo
EGYPT
SAUDI ARABIA
Neutral until Mar. 1945

SCALE OF MILES
0 100 200 300 400 500
© Copyright HAMMOND INCORPORATED, Maplewood, N.J.

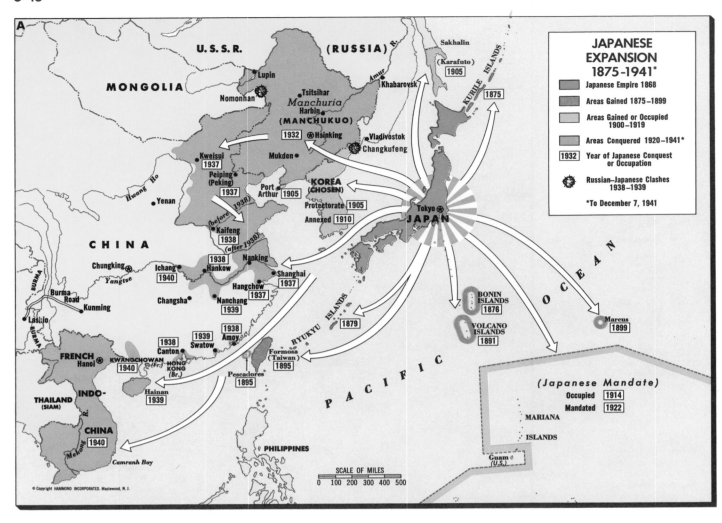

A

JAPANESE EXPANSION 1875-1941*

- Japanese Empire 1868
- Areas Gained 1875-1899
- Areas Gained or Occupied 1900-1919
- Areas Conquered 1920-1941*
- 1932 Year of Japanese Conquest or Occupation
- ❂ Russian-Japanese Clashes 1938-1939

*To December 7, 1941

U.S.S.R. (RUSSIA)

MONGOLIA

Sakhalin (Karafuto) 1905

KURILE ISLANDS 1875

•Lupin
•Nomonhan ❂
•Tsitsihar
Harbin
Manchuria (MANCHUKUO)
Khabarovsk
Amur R.

1932 ❂ Hsinking
Vladivostok
Changkufeng ❂
Mukden

Kweisui 1937
Peiping (Peking)•
1937
Port Arthur 1905
KOREA (CHOSEN)
Protectorate 1905
Annexed 1910

Tokyo ❂ JAPAN

Hwang Ho
•Yenan
Kaifeng 1938
(before 1938)

CHINA
Chungking ⊗
Ichang 1940
(after 1938)
1938
Hankow
Nanking
Shanghai 1937
Hangchow 1937
Nanchang 1939
Changsha•
Yangtse

BONIN ISLANDS 1876

VOLCANO ISLANDS 1891

Marcus 1899

RYUKYU ISLANDS 1879

BURMA
Burma Road
Kunming
•Lashio
BURMA

1939 1938
Swatow
1938 Canton
Amoy
KWANGCHOWAN (Fr.) 1940
HONG KONG (Br.)
Pescadores 1895

Formosa (Taiwan) 1895

FRENCH Hanoi ⊗
THAILAND (SIAM)
INDO-
Hainan 1939

CHINA 1940
Mekong R.
Camranh Bay

PHILIPPINES

PACIFIC OCEAN

(Japanese Mandate)
Occupied 1914
Mandated 1922

MARIANA ISLANDS

Guam (U.S.)

SCALE OF MILES
0 100 200 300 400 500

© Copyright HAMMOND INCORPORATED, Maplewood, N.J.

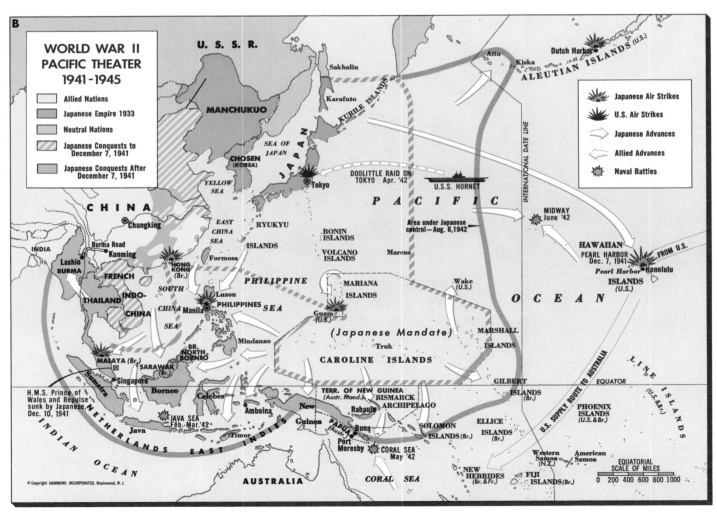

B

WORLD WAR II PACIFIC THEATER 1941-1945

- Allied Nations
- Japanese Empire 1933
- Neutral Nations
- Japanese Conquests to December 7, 1941
- Japanese Conquests After December 7, 1941

- ✸ Japanese Air Strikes
- ✸ U.S. Air Strikes
- ⇨ Japanese Advances
- ⇦ Allied Advances
- ✸ Naval Battles

U.S.S.R.

MANCHUKUO
Sakhalin
Karafuto
KURILE ISLANDS
SEA OF JAPAN

Attu
Kiska
Dutch Harbor (U.S.)
ALEUTIAN ISLANDS (U.S.)

CHOSEN (KOREA)

YELLOW SEA

CHINA
⊗ Chungking

JAPAN ❂ Tokyo

DOOLITTLE RAID ON TOKYO Apr. '42
U.S.S. HORNET

INTERNATIONAL DATE LINE

EAST CHINA SEA
RYUKYU ISLANDS

PACIFIC OCEAN

MIDWAY June '42

Area under Japanese control—Aug. 6,1942

HAWAIIAN
PEARL HARBOR Dec. 7, 1941
Pearl Harbor ✸ Honolulu
ISLANDS (U.S.)

FROM U.S.

BONIN ISLANDS
VOLCANO ISLANDS
Marcus

INDIA
Burma Road
Lashio Kunming
BURMA
FRENCH
THAILAND
INDO-
CHINA

HONG KONG (Br.)
Formosa

SOUTH CHINA SEA

Luzon
PHILIPPINES
Manila
PHILIPPINE SEA

MARIANA ISLANDS
Guam (U.S.)

Wake (U.S.)

MALAYA (Br.)
SARAWAK (Br.)
Singapore
BR. NORTH BORNEO
Borneo

Mindanao

(Japanese Mandate)
Truk
CAROLINE ISLANDS

MARSHALL ISLANDS

H.M.S. Prince of Wales and Repulse sunk by Japanese, Dec. 10, 1941

Sumatra
NETHERLANDS
JAVA SEA Feb.-Mar.'42
Java
Celebes
Amboina
Timor

EAST INDIES
Port Moresby
CORAL SEA May '42

New Guinea
PAPUA (Austr.)
Buna

TERR. OF NEW GUINEA (Austr. Mand.)
BISMARCK ARCHIPELAGO
Rabaul

SOLOMON ISLANDS (Br.)

GILBERT ISLANDS (Br.)

EQUATOR

ELLICE ISLANDS (Br.)

U.S. SUPPLY ROUTE TO AUSTRALIA

PHOENIX ISLANDS (U.S. & Br.)

LINE ISLANDS (U.S. & Br.)

INDIAN OCEAN

AUSTRALIA

CORAL SEA

NEW HEBRIDES (Br. & Fr.)
FIJI ISLANDS (Br.)

Western Samoa (N.Z.)
American Samoa

EQUATORIAL SCALE OF MILES
0 200 400 600 800 1000

© Copyright HAMMOND INCORPORATED, Maplewood, N.J.

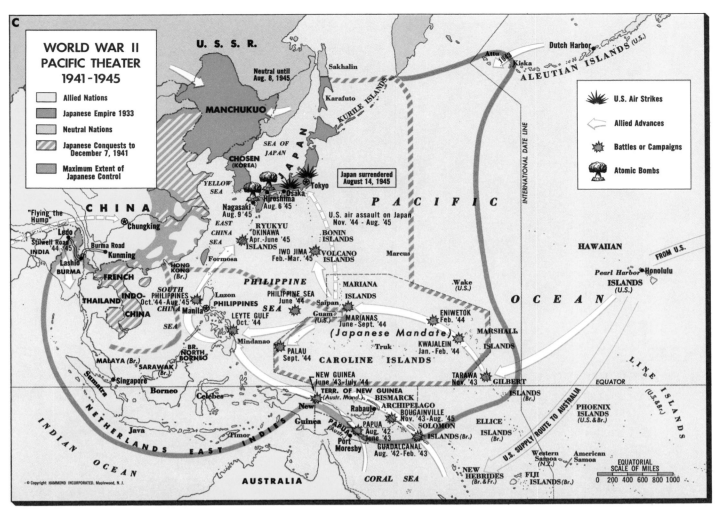

C

WORLD WAR II PACIFIC THEATER 1941-1945

- Allied Nations
- Japanese Empire 1933
- Neutral Nations
- Japanese Conquests to December 7, 1941
- Maximum Extent of Japanese Control

- ★ U.S. Air Strikes
- ⇦ Allied Advances
- ✴ Battles or Campaigns
- ☁ Atomic Bombs

U. S. S. R.

Sakhalin

Attu 1943

Kiska

Dutch Harbor (U.S.)

ALEUTIAN ISLANDS

Karafuto

Neutral until Aug. 8, 1945

MANCHUKUO

KURILE ISLANDS

INTERNATIONAL DATE LINE

SEA OF JAPAN

JAPAN

CHOSEN (KOREA)

Tokyo

Japan surrendered August 14, 1945

YELLOW SEA

Osaka

Hiroshima Aug. 6 '45

P A C I F I C

"Flying the Hump"

C H I N A

Chungking

Ledo

Stilwell Road '44-'45

Nagasaki Aug. 9 '45

EAST CHINA SEA

RYUKYU OKINAWA Apr.-June '45 ISLANDS

U.S. air assault on Japan Nov. '44 - Aug. '45

BONIN ISLANDS

INDIA

Burma Road

Kunming

Lashio

BURMA

Formosa

IWO JIMA Feb.-Mar. '45

VOLCANO ISLANDS

Marcus

HAWAIIAN

FROM U.S.

FRENCH

HONG KONG (Br.)

PHILIPPINE

SOUTH PHILIPPINES Oct.'44-Aug.'45

Luzon

PHILIPPINES

PHILIPPINE SEA June '44

MARIANA ISLANDS

Wake (U.S.)

O C E A N

Pearl Harbor Honolulu

ISLANDS (U.S.)

INDO-

CHINA

THAILAND

Manila

SEA

LEYTE GULF Oct. '44

Saipan

Guam (U.S.)

MARIANAS June-Sept. '44

ENIWETOK Feb. '44

MARSHALL ISLANDS

Mindanao

(Japanese Mandate)

KWAJALEIN Jan.-Feb. '44

MALAYA (Br.)

BR. NORTH BORNEO

PALAU Sept. '44

Truk

SARAWAK (Br.)

CAROLINE ISLANDS

Sumatra

Singapore

Borneo

Celebes

TARAWA Nov. '43

GILBERT

EQUATOR

LINE ISLANDS (U.S.& Br.)

NETHERLANDS EAST INDIES

Java

Timor

NEW GUINEA June '43-July '44

TERR. OF NEW GUINEA (Austr. Mand.)

ISLANDS (Br.)

U.S. SUPPLY ROUTE TO AUSTRALIA

PHOENIX ISLANDS (U.S. & Br.)

INDIAN

OCEAN

New Guinea

Rabaul

BISMARCK ARCHIPELAGO

BOUGAINVILLE Nov. '43-Aug. '45

PAPUA Aug. '42-June '43

SOLOMON ISLANDS (Br.)

ELLICE ISLANDS (Br.)

Western Samoa (N.Z.)

American Samoa

Port Moresby

GUADALCANAL Aug. '42-Feb. '43

EQUATORIAL SCALE OF MILES

AUSTRALIA

CORAL SEA

NEW HEBRIDES (Br. & Fr.)

FIJI ISLANDS (Br.)

0 200 400 600 800 1000

© Copyright HAMMOND INCORPORATED, Maplewood, N.J.

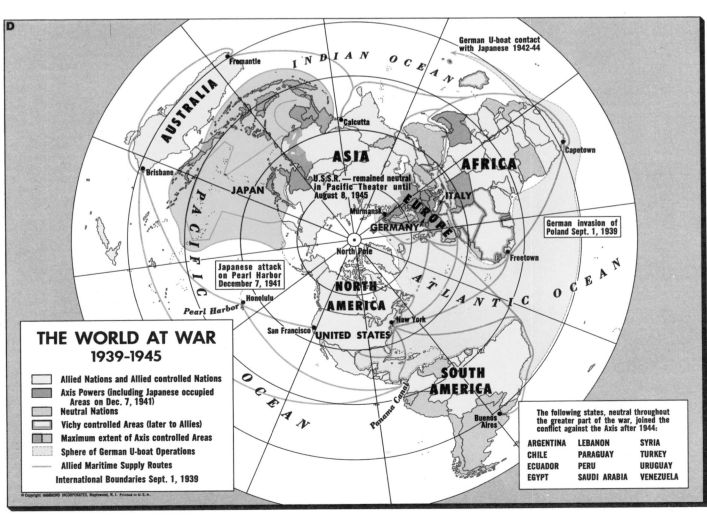

D

German U-boat contact with Japanese 1942-44

INDIAN OCEAN

Fremantle

AUSTRALIA

Calcutta

Capetown

ASIA

AFRICA

PACIFIC

JAPAN

Brisbane

U.S.S.R. — remained neutral in Pacific Theater until August 8, 1945

ITALY

EUROPE

German invasion of Poland Sept. 1, 1939

Murmansk

GERMANY

North Pole

Freetown

Japanese attack on Pearl Harbor December 7, 1941

Honolulu

NORTH AMERICA

ATLANTIC OCEAN

Pearl Harbor

San Francisco

UNITED STATES

New York

OCEAN

THE WORLD AT WAR 1939-1945

- Allied Nations and Allied controlled Nations
- Axis Powers (including Japanese occupied Areas on Dec. 7, 1941)
- Neutral Nations
- Vichy controlled Areas (later to Allies)
- Maximum extent of Axis controlled Areas
- Sphere of German U-boat Operations
- Allied Maritime Supply Routes
- International Boundaries Sept. 1, 1939

SOUTH AMERICA

Panama Canal

Buenos Aires

The following states, neutral throughout the greater part of the war, joined the conflict against the Axis after 1944:

ARGENTINA	LEBANON	SYRIA
CHILE	PARAGUAY	TURKEY
ECUADOR	PERU	URUGUAY
EGYPT	SAUDI ARABIA	VENEZUELA

© Copyright HAMMOND INCORPORATED, Maplewood, N.J. Printed in U.S.A.

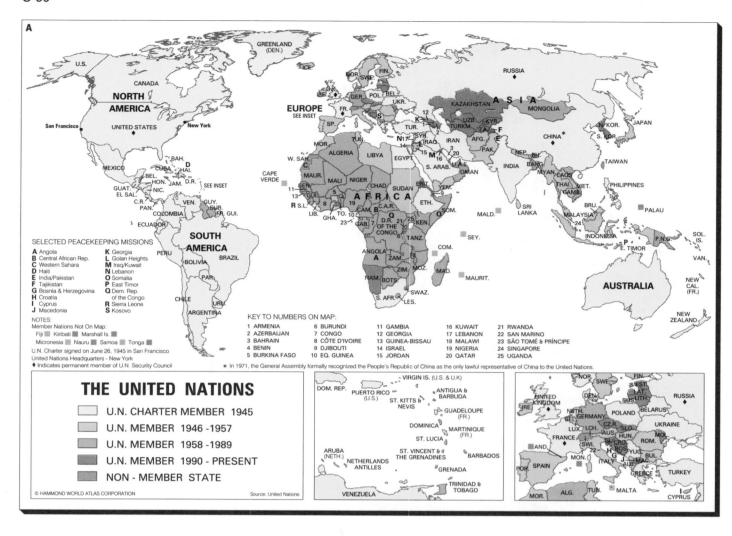

A

GREENLAND (DEN.)

U.S. CANADA

NORTH AMERICA

UNITED STATES

San Francisco ◆ New York

MEXICO
BAH. D
CUBA HAI.
BEL. JAM. D.R.
GUAT. HON. SEE INSET
EL SAL. NIC.
C.R. VEN. GUY.
PAN. SUR.
COLOMBIA FR. GUI.
ECUADOR
PERU
SOUTH AMERICA
BOLIVIA BRAZIL
PAR.
CHILE URU.
ARGENTINA

ICE.
NOR. FIN. SWE.
EUROPE SEE INSET
GER. POL. BEL.
FR. UKR.
SP. S
TUR.
N17 SYR. IRAQ
14 15 M
MOR. TUN. 16 20
ALGERIA LIBYA EGYPT S. ARAB. U.A.E. OMAN
W. SAH.
CAPE VERDE C
MAUR. MALI NIGER CHAD SUDAN ERIT. YEM.
SEN. 11 5 19 ETH.
13 GUI. CAM. C.A.R. O SOM.
R S.L. LIB. GHA. TO. 10 B Q 21 KEN.
23 GAB. 7 D.R. OF THE CONGO TANZ.
ANGOLA A ZAM.
NAM. ZIM. MOZ.
BOTS. SWAZ.
S. AFR. LES.

RUSSIA ◆

KAZAKHSTAN ASIA MONGOLIA
UZB. KYR.
TURKM. TAJ. F
AFG. E
PAK. CHINA * ◆ N. KOR. JAPAN
NEP. BH. S. KOR.
INDIA BANG. MYAN. LAOS TAIWAN
THAI. VIET.
SRI LANKA CAMB. PHILIPPINES
MALD. BRU. PALAU
MALAYSIA 24
INDONESIA P E. TIMOR P.N.G. SOL. IS.
SEY. VAN.
COM. NEW CAL. (FR.)
MAD. AUSTRALIA
MAURIT. NEW ZEALAND

SELECTED PEACEKEEPING MISSIONS

A Angola
B Central African Rep.
C Western Sahara
D Haiti
E India/Pakistan
F Tajikistan
G Bosnia & Herzegovina
H Croatia
I Cyprus
J Macedonia
K Georgia
L Golan Heights
M Iraq/Kuwait
N Lebanon
O Somalia
P East Timor
Q Dem. Rep. of the Congo
R Sierra Leone
S Kosovo

NOTES:
Member Nations Not On Map:
Fiji ▪ Kiribati ▪ Marshall Is. ▪
Micronesia ▪ Nauru ▪ Samoa ▪ Tonga ▪
U.N. Charter signed on June 26, 1945 in San Francisco
United Nations Headquarters - New York
◆ Indicates permanent member of U.N. Security Council

KEY TO NUMBERS ON MAP:

1 ARMENIA
2 AZERBAIJAN
3 BAHRAIN
4 BENIN
5 BURKINA FASO
6 BURUNDI
7 CONGO
8 CÔTE D'IVOIRE
9 DJIBOUTI
10 EQ. GUINEA
11 GAMBIA
12 GEORGIA
13 GUINEA-BISSAU
14 ISRAEL
15 JORDAN
16 KUWAIT
17 LEBANON
18 MALAWI
19 NIGERIA
20 QATAR
21 RWANDA
22 SAN MARINO
23 SÃO TOMÉ & PRÍNCIPE
24 SINGAPORE
25 UGANDA

* In 1971, the General Assembly formally recognized the People's Republic of China as the only lawful representative of China to the United Nations.

THE UNITED NATIONS

▫ U.N. CHARTER MEMBER 1945
▫ U.N. MEMBER 1946 -1957
▫ U.N. MEMBER 1958 -1989
▪ U.N. MEMBER 1990 - PRESENT
▪ NON - MEMBER STATE

© HAMMOND WORLD ATLAS CORPORATION   Source: United Nations

VIRGIN IS. (U.S. & U.K)
DOM. REP. PUERTO RICO (U.S.)
ANTIGUA & BARBUDA
ST. KITTS & NEVIS
GUADELOUPE (FR.)
DOMINICA
MARTINIQUE (FR.)
ST. LUCIA
ARUBA (NETH.) ST. VINCENT & THE GRENADINES BARBADOS
NETHERLANDS ANTILLES
GRENADA
TRINIDAD & TOBAGO
VENEZUELA

NOR. FIN. SWE. EST. LAT. LITH.
UNITED KINGDOM DEN. RUSSIA
IRE. NETH. GERMANY POLAND BELARUS
BEL. LUX. LCH. CZ.R. SLO. UKRAINE
FRANCE SWI. AUS. HUN. ROM.
AND. SL. CRO. BOS. YUG. BUL.
MON. I. MAC.
POR. SPAIN ITALY ALB. GREECE TURKEY
MOR. ALG. TUN. MALTA I CYPRUS

B

GREENLAND (DEN.)

U.S. CANADA

NORTH AMERICA

UNITED STATES

MEXICO
BAH.
CUBA HAI.
BEL. JAM. D.R.
GUAT. HON.
EL SAL. NIC.
C.R. VEN. GUY.
PAN. SUR.
COLOMBIA FR. GUI.
ECUADOR
PERU
SOUTH AMERICA
BOLIVIA BRAZIL
PAR.
CHILE URU.
ARGENTINA

ICE.
NOR. FIN. SWE.
IRE.
EUROPE SEE INSET
GER. POL. BEL.
FR. UKR.
SP.
TUR.
17 SYR. IRAQ
MOR. TUN. 14 15
ALGERIA LIBYA EGYPT 16 20
W. SAH. S. ARAB. U.A.E. OMAN
CAPE VERDE
MAUR. MALI NIGER CHAD SUDAN ERIT. YEM.
SEN. 11 5 19 ETH.
13 GUI. CAM. C.A.R. SOM.
S.L. LIB. GHA. TO. 10 21 KEN.
22 GAB. 7 D.R. OF THE CONGO TANZ.
ANGOLA ZAM.
NAM. ZIM. MOZ.
BOTS. SWAZ.
S. AFR. LES.

RUSSIA
KAZAKHSTAN ASIA MONGOLIA
UZB. KYR.
TURKM. TAJ.
AFG.
PAK. CHINA N. KOR. JAPAN
NEP. BH. S. KOR.
INDIA BANG. MYAN. LAOS TAIWAN
THAI. VIET.
SRI LANKA CAMB. PHILIPPINES
MALD. BRU. PALAU
MALAYSIA 23
INDONESIA E. TIMOR P.N.G. SOL. IS.
SEY. VAN.
COM. NEW CAL. (FR.)
MAD. AUSTRALIA
MAURIT. NEW ZEALAND

NOTES:
* Status Of Nations Not On Map:
Fiji ▪ Marshall Islands ▪ Micronesia ▪ Samoa ▪
Kiribati ▪ Nauru ▪ Tonga ▪ Tuvalu ▪
* U.S. is a member of OAS, NATO and ANZUS.
* Canada is a member of OAS and NATO.
* Antigua & Barbuda, Barbados, Dominica, Grenada,
St. Lucia, St. Vincent & the Grenadines, St. Kitts & Nevis
and Trindad & Tobago are also members of the OAS.

KEY TO NUMBERS ON MAP:

1 ARMENIA
2 AZERBAIJAN
3 BAHRAIN
4 BENIN
5 BURKINA FASO
6 BURUNDI
7 CONGO
8 CÔTE D'IVOIRE
9 DJIBOUTI
10 EQ. GUINEA
11 GAMBIA
12 GEORGIA
13 GUINEA-BISSAU
14 ISRAEL
15 JORDAN
16 KUWAIT
17 LEBANON
18 MALAWI
19 NIGERIA
20 QATAR
21 RWANDA
22 SÃO TOMÉ & PRÍNCIPE
23 SINGAPORE
24 UGANDA

U.S. and WORLD ALLIANCES

▪ ORGANIZATION OF AMERICAN STATES (OAS)
▪ NORTH ATLANTIC TREATY ORGANIZATION (NATO)
▪ ANZUS PACT (ANZUS)
▪ BILATERAL TREATIES WITH U.S.
▫ MULTIPLE ALLIANCE NATIONS

▪ COMMUNIST NATIONS
▫ FORMER COMMUNIST NATIONS
(Czech Republic, Hungary, and Poland
were also Communist nations before 1989)
▫ FORMER U.S.S.R.
▪ NON - ALLIANCE NATIONS

© HAMMOND WORLD ATLAS CORPORATION   Source: C.I.A. World Factbook

NOR. FIN. SWE. EST. LAT. LITH.
UNITED KINGDOM DEN. RUSSIA
IRE. NETH. GERMANY POLAND BELARUS
BEL. LUX. CZ.R. SLO. UKRAINE
FRANCE SWI. AUS. HUN. ROM.
SL. CRO. BOS. YUG. MOL.
ALB. BUL.
POR. SPAIN ITALY GREECE TURKEY
MOR. ALG. TUN. Andorra, Malta, and Monaco
are not members of NATO. CYPRUS

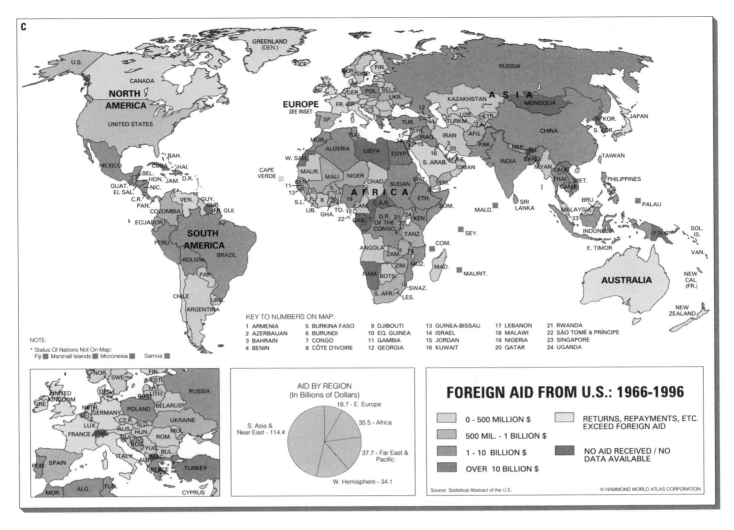

C

KEY TO NUMBERS ON MAP:

1 ARMENIA	5 BURKINA FASO	9 DJIBOUTI	13 GUINEA-BISSAU	17 LEBANON	21 RWANDA
2 AZERBAIJAN	6 BURUNDI	10 EQ. GUINEA	14 ISRAEL	18 MALAWI	22 SÃO TOMÉ & PRÍNCIPE
3 BAHRAIN	7 CONGO	11 GAMBIA	15 JORDAN	19 NIGERIA	23 SINGAPORE
4 BENIN	8 CÔTE D'IVOIRE	12 GEORGIA	16 KUWAIT	20 QATAR	24 UGANDA

NOTE:
* Status Of Nations Not On Map:
Fiji ▓ Marshall Islands ▓ Micronesia ▓ Samoa ▓

AID BY REGION
(In Billions of Dollars)

18.7 - E. Europe
35.5 - Africa
S. Asia & Near East - 114.4
37.7 - Far East & Pacific
W. Hemisphere - 34.1

FOREIGN AID FROM U.S.: 1966-1996

- 0 - 500 MILLION $
- 500 MIL. - 1 BILLION $
- 1 - 10 BILLION $
- OVER 10 BILLION $
- RETURNS, REPAYMENTS, ETC. EXCEED FOREIGN AID
- NO AID RECEIVED / NO DATA AVAILABLE

Source: Statistical Abstract of the U.S.

© HAMMOND WORLD ATLAS CORPORATION

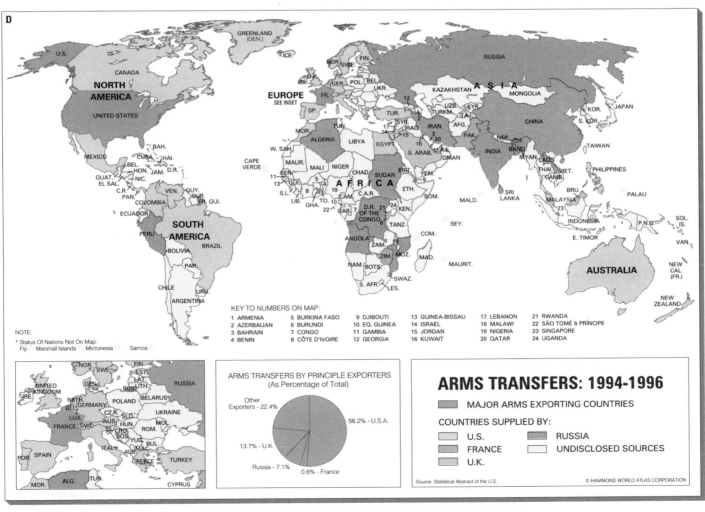

D

KEY TO NUMBERS ON MAP:

1 ARMENIA	5 BURKINA FASO	9 DJIBOUTI	13 GUINEA-BISSAU	17 LEBANON	21 RWANDA
2 AZERBAIJAN	6 BURUNDI	10 EQ. GUINEA	14 ISRAEL	18 MALAWI	22 SÃO TOMÉ & PRÍNCIPE
3 BAHRAIN	7 CONGO	11 GAMBIA	15 JORDAN	19 NIGERIA	23 SINGAPORE
4 BENIN	8 CÔTE D'IVOIRE	12 GEORGIA	16 KUWAIT	20 QATAR	24 UGANDA

NOTE:
* Status Of Nations Not On Map:
Fiji ▓ Marshall Islands ▓ Micronesia ▓ Samoa ▓

ARMS TRANSFERS BY PRINCIPLE EXPORTERS
(As Percentage of Total)

Other Exporters - 22.4%
56.2% - U.S.A.
13.7% - U.K.
Russia - 7.1%
0.6% - France

ARMS TRANSFERS: 1994-1996

MAJOR ARMS EXPORTING COUNTRIES

COUNTRIES SUPPLIED BY:
- U.S.
- FRANCE
- U.K.
- RUSSIA
- UNDISCLOSED SOURCES

Source: Statistical Abstract of the U.S.

© HAMMOND WORLD ATLAS CORPORATION

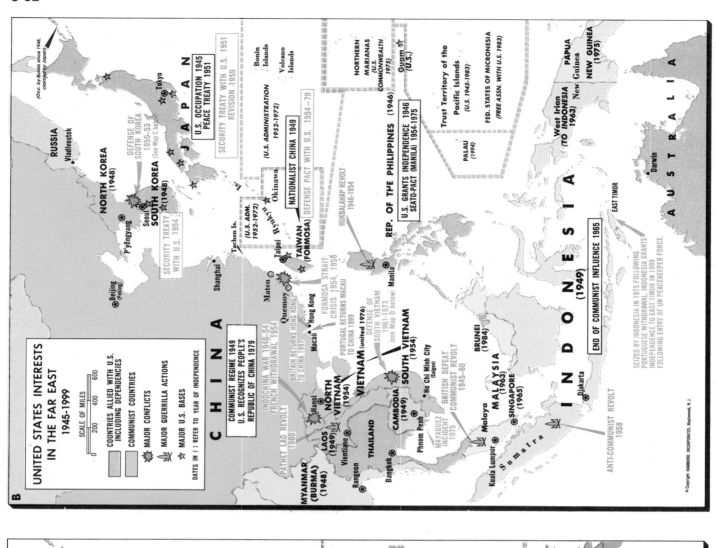

UNITED STATES INTERESTS IN THE FAR EAST 1945–1999

SCALE OF MILES
0   200   400   600

COUNTRIES ALLIED WITH U.S. INCLUDING DEPENDENCIES

COMMUNIST COUNTRIES

✸ MAJOR CONFLICTS

MAJOR GUERRILLA ACTIONS

☆ MAJOR U.S. BASES

DATES IN ( ) REFER TO YEAR OF INDEPENDENCE

COMMUNIST REGIME 1949
U.S. RECOGNIZES PEOPLES REPUBLIC OF CHINA 1979

RUSSIA
Vladivostok

(Occ. by Russia since 1945, claimed by Japan)

JAPAN
Tokyo

U.S. OCCUPATION 1945
PEACE TREATY 1951

SECURITY TREATY WITH U.S. 1951
REVISION 1959

(U.S. ADMINISTRATION 1952-1972)

Bonin Islands
Volcano Islands

NORTH KOREA (1948)
Pyŏngyang

DEFENSE OF SOUTH KOREA 1950-53 (See Map C)

SOUTH KOREA (1948)
Seoul

SECURITY TREATY WITH U.S. 1954

NATIONALIST CHINA 1949
DEFENSE PACT WITH U.S. 1954-79

(U.S. ADM. 1952-1972) Ryukyus

Okinawa

NORTHERN MARIANAS (U.S. COMMONWEALTH 1975)
Guam (U.S.)

Trust Territory of the Pacific Islands (U.S. 1945-1983)

PALAU (1994)

FED. STATES OF MICRONESIA (FREE ASSN. WITH U.S. 1983)

CHINA
Beijing (Peking)
Shanghai

Tachen Is.

TAIWAN (FORMOSA)
Taipei

FORMOSA STRAIT CRISIS 1954, 1958

Quemoy
Matsu

BRITAIN RETURNS HONG KONG TO CHINA 1997
Hong Kong
Macau

PORTUGAL RETURNS MACAU TO CHINA 1999

REP. OF THE PHILIPPINES (1946)
Manila

U.S. GRANTS PHILIPPINE INDEPENDENCE 1946
SEATO-PACT (MANILA) 1954-1975

West Irian (TO INDONESIA 1963) New Guinea

PAPUA NEW GUINEA (1975)

INDOCHINA WAR 1946-54
FRENCH WITHDRAWAL 1954

PATHET LAO REVOLT 1960

MYANMAR (BURMA) (1948)
Rangoon

LAOS (1949)
Vientiane

Hanoi
NORTH VIETNAM (1954)

VIETNAM (united 1976)

DEFENSE OF SOUTH VIETNAM 1961-1973 (see Map D below)

SOUTH VIETNAM (1954)
Ho Chi Minh City (Saigon)

THAILAND
Bangkok

CAMBODIA (1949)
Phnom Penh

MAYAGUEZ INCIDENT 1975

BRITISH DEFEAT COMMUNIST REVOLT 1945-60

BRUNEI (1984)

MALAYSIA (1963)
Malaya

SINGAPORE (1965)
Kuala Lumpur

Sumatra

INDONESIA (1949)
Djakarta

END OF COMMUNIST INFLUENCE 1965

AUSTRALIA
Darwin

EAST TIMOR

ANTI-COMMUNIST REVOLT 1958

SEIZED BY INDONESIA IN 1975 FOLLOWING PORTUGUESE WITHDRAWAL. INDONESIA GRANTS INDEPENDENCE TO EAST TIMOR IN 1999 FOLLOWING ENTRY OF UN PEACEKEEPER FORCE.

© Copyright HAMMOND INCORPORATED, Maplewood, N.J.

B

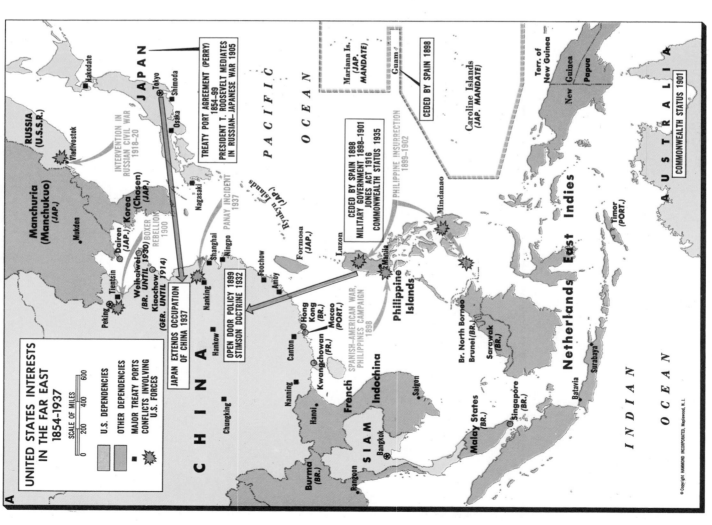

UNITED STATES INTERESTS IN THE FAR EAST 1854–1937

SCALE OF MILES
0   200   400   600

U.S. DEPENDENCIES

OTHER DEPENDENCIES

■ MAJOR TREATY PORTS

✸ CONFLICTS INVOLVING U.S. FORCES

RUSSIA (U.S.S.R.)
Vladivostok

INTERVENTION IN RUSSIAN CIVIL WAR 1918-20

JAPAN
Tokyo
Hakodate
Shimoda
Osaka
Nagasaki

TREATY PORT AGREEMENT (PERRY) 1854-99
PRESIDENT T. ROOSEVELT MEDIATES IN RUSSIAN–JAPANESE WAR 1905

PANAY INCIDENT 1937

Manchuria (Manchukuo) (JAP.)
Mukden

Korea (Chosen) (JAP.)

Dairen (JAP.)
Weihaiwei (BR. UNTIL 1930)
Kiaochow (GER. UNTIL 1914)

BOXER REBELLION 1900

Tientsin
Peking

CHINA
Hankow
Nanking
Shanghai
Ningpo
Foochow
Amoy

Chungking

Canton

Hong Kong (BR.)
Macao (PORT.)
Kwangchowan (FR.)

Namning

OPEN DOOR POLICY 1899
STIMSON DOCTRINE 1932

JAPAN EXTENDS OCCUPATION OF CHINA 1937

Formosa (JAP.)

Ryukyu Islands (JAP.)

Mariana Is. (JAP. MANDATE)
Guam

CEDED BY SPAIN 1898

Caroline Islands (JAP. MANDATE)

PACIFIC OCEAN

CEDED BY SPAIN 1898
MILITARY GOVERNMENT 1898-1901
JONES ACT 1916
COMMONWEALTH STATUS 1935

Luzon
Manila
Mindanao

PHILIPPINE INSURRECTION 1899-1902

Philippine Islands

SPANISH-AMERICAN WAR, PHILIPPINES CAMPAIGN 1898

SIAM
Bangkok

Burma (BR.)
Rangoon

French Indochina
Hanoi
Saigon

Malay States (BR.)
Singapore (BR.)

Br. North Borneo (BR.)
Brunei (BR.)
Sarawak (BR.)

Netherlands East Indies
Batavia
Surabaya

Timor (PORT.)

New Guinea
Terr. of New Guinea
Papua

AUSTRALIA

COMMONWEALTH STATUS 1901

INDIAN OCEAN

© Copyright HAMMOND INCORPORATED, Maplewood, N.J.

A

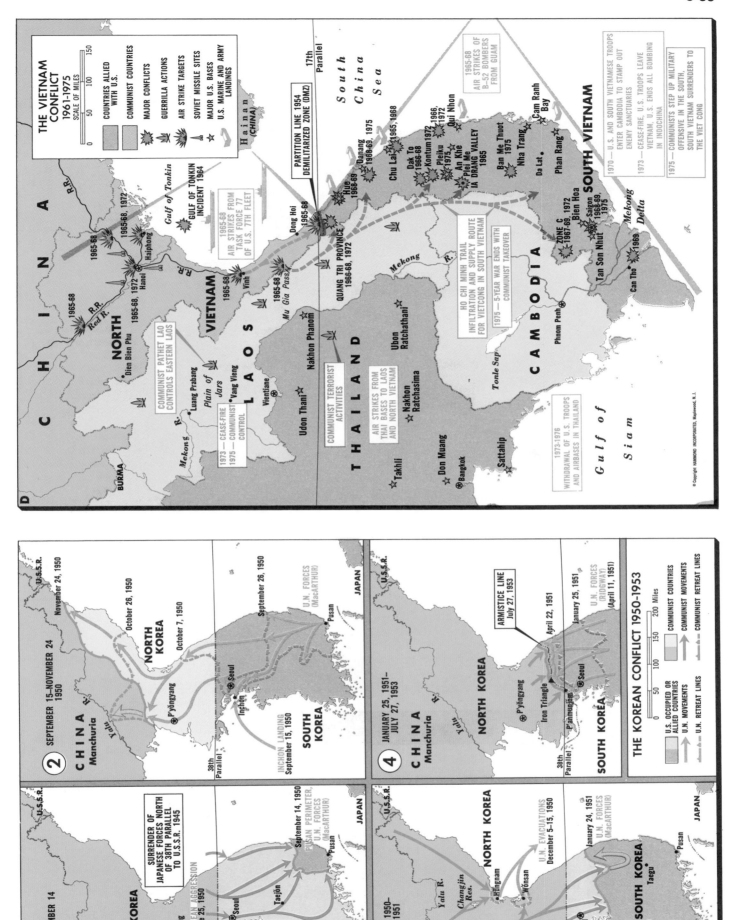

THE VIETNAM CONFLICT 1961-1975

SCALE OF MILES
0   100   150

COUNTRIES ALLIED WITH U.S.

COMMUNIST COUNTRIES

MAJOR CONFLICTS

GUERRILLA ACTIONS

AIR STRIKE TARGETS

SOVIET MISSILE SITES

MAJOR U.S. BASES

U.S. MARINE AND ARMY LANDINGS

1965-68 AIR STRIKES OF B-52 BOMBERS FROM GUAM

1970 — U.S. AND SOUTH VIETNAMESE TROOPS ENTER CAMBODIA TO STAMP OUT ENEMY SANCTUARIES

1973 — CEASE-FIRE, U.S. TROOPS LEAVE VIETNAM, U.S. ENDS ALL BOMBING IN INDOCHINA

1975 — COMMUNISTS STEP UP MILITARY OFFENSIVE IN THE SOUTH, SOUTH VIETNAM SURRENDERS TO THE VIET CONG

1965-68 AIR STRIKES FROM TASK FORCE 77 OF U.S. 7TH FLEET

GULF OF TONKIN INCIDENT 1964

PARTITION LINE 1954 DEMILITARIZED ZONE (DMZ)

17th Parallel

South China Sea

Hainan (CHINA)

Gulf of Tonkin

C H I N A

R.R.

Red R.

R.R.

Dien Bien Phu

NORTH VIETNAM

1965-68, 1972

Hanoi Haiphong

1965-68

Vinh

Dong Hoi

1965-68

Mu Gia Pass

COMMUNIST PATHET LAO CONTROLS EASTERN LAOS

Luang Prabang

Plain of Jars

Yang Vieng

1973 — CEASE-FIRE
1975 — COMMUNIST CONTROL

L A O S

Vientiane

Mekong R.

Udon Thani

Nakhon Phanom

COMMUNIST TERRORIST ACTIVITIES

AIR STRIKES FROM THAI BASES TO LAOS AND NORTH VIETNAM

T H A I L A N D

Ubon Ratchathani

Nakhon Ratchasima

Takhli

Don Muang

Bangkok

Sattahip

Gulf of Siam

QUANG TRI PROVINCE 1966-68, 1972

Hue 1968-69

Danang 1968-69, 1975

Chu Lai

Dak To 1966-68

Kontum 1972

Pleiku 1966, 1972

An Khe

Plei Me 1965

IA DRANG VALLEY 1965

Qui Nhon

Ban Me Thuot 1975

Nha Trang

Cam Ranh Bay

Da Lat

Phan Rang

SOUTH VIETNAM

HO CHI MINH TRAIL INFILTRATION AND SUPPLY ROUTE FOR VIETCONG IN SOUTH VIETNAM

1975 — 5-YEAR WAR ENDS WITH COMMUNIST TAKEOVER

Mekong R.

C A M B O D I A

Phnom Penh

Tonle Sap

ZONE C 1967-69, 1972

Bien Hoa

Saigon 1968-69, 1975

Tan Son Nhut

Can Tho 1969

Mekong Delta

BURMA

Mekong R.

1973-1976 WITHDRAWAL OF U.S. TROOPS AND AIRBASES IN THAILAND

© Copyright HAMMOND INCORPORATED, Maplewood, N.J.

THE KOREAN CONFLICT 1950-1953

U.S. OCCUPIED OR ALLIED COUNTRIES

U.N. MOVEMENTS

U.N. RETREAT LINES

COMMUNIST COUNTRIES

COMMUNIST MOVEMENTS

COMMUNIST RETREAT LINES

0   50   100   150   200 Miles

① JUNE 25-SEPTEMBER 14 1950

C H I N A
Manchuria

Yalu R.

U.S.S.R.

NORTH KOREA

Pyŏngyang

SURRENDER OF JAPANESE FORCES NORTH OF 38TH PARALLEL TO U.S.S.R. 1945

38th Parallel

NORTH KOREAN AGGRESSION June 25, 1950

Seoul

SOUTH KOREA

Taejŏn

SURRENDER OF JAPANESE FORCES SOUTH OF 38TH PARALLEL TO U.S. 1945

PUSAN PERIMETER, U.N. FORCES (MacARTHUR) September 14, 1950

Pusan

Mokpo

JAPAN

© Copyright HAMMOND INCORPORATED, Maplewood, N.J.

② SEPTEMBER 15-NOVEMBER 24 1950

U.S.S.R.

November 24, 1950

October 26, 1950

C H I N A
Manchuria

Yalu R.

NORTH KOREA

October 7, 1950

Pyŏngyang

Seoul

INCHON LANDING September 15, 1950

Inchon

SOUTH KOREA

September 26, 1950

Pusan

U.N. FORCES (MacARTHUR)

JAPAN

③ NOVEMBER 25, 1950- JANUARY 24, 1951

C H I N A
Manchuria

Yalu R.

CHINESE INTERVENTION November 1950

U.S.S.R.

Changjin Res.

NORTH KOREA

Hŭngnam

Wŏnsan

U.N. EVACUATIONS December 5-15, 1950

Pyŏngyang

Seoul

SOUTH KOREA

Taegu

January 24, 1951

U.N. FORCES (MacARTHUR)

Pusan

JAPAN

④ JANUARY 25, 1951- JULY 27, 1953

C H I N A
Manchuria

Yalu R.

U.S.S.R.

ARMISTICE LINE July 27, 1953

April 22, 1951

NORTH KOREA

P'yŏngyang

Iron Triangle

P'anmunjŏm

January 25, 1951

38th Parallel

Seoul

SOUTH KOREA

U.N. FORCES (RIDGWAY) (April 11, 1951)

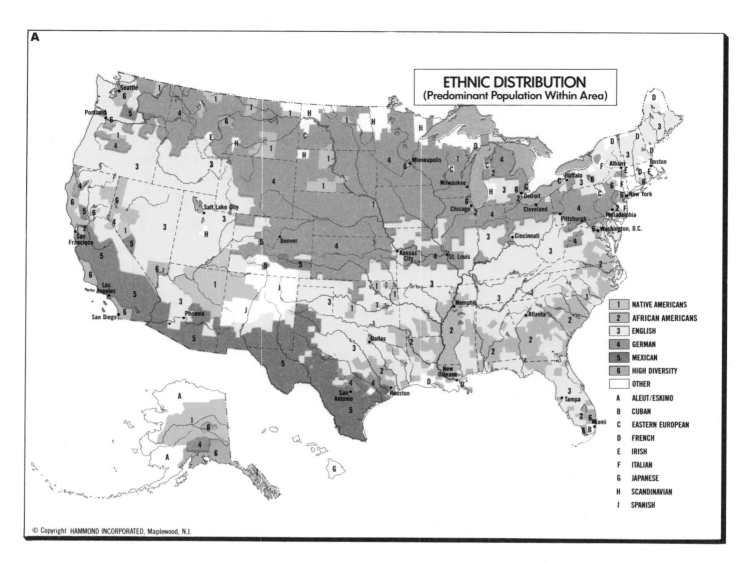

ETHNIC DISTRIBUTION
(Predominant Population Within Area)

1	NATIVE AMERICANS
2	AFRICAN AMERICANS
3	ENGLISH
4	GERMAN
5	MEXICAN
6	HIGH DIVERSITY
	OTHER
A	ALEUT/ESKIMO
B	CUBAN
C	EASTERN EUROPEAN
D	FRENCH
E	IRISH
F	ITALIAN
G	JAPANESE
H	SCANDINAVIAN
J	SPANISH

© Copyright HAMMOND INCORPORATED, Maplewood, N.J.

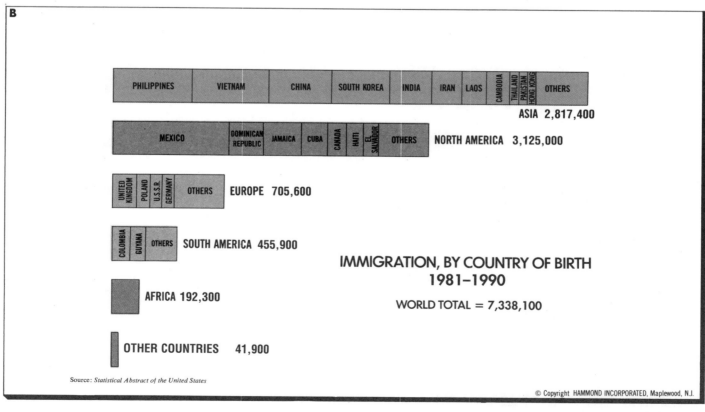

IMMIGRATION, BY COUNTRY OF BIRTH
1981–1990

ASIA 2,817,400

NORTH AMERICA 3,125,000

EUROPE 705,600

SOUTH AMERICA 455,900

AFRICA 192,300

OTHER COUNTRIES 41,900

WORLD TOTAL = 7,338,100

Source: *Statistical Abstract of the United States*

© Copyright HAMMOND INCORPORATED, Maplewood, N.J.

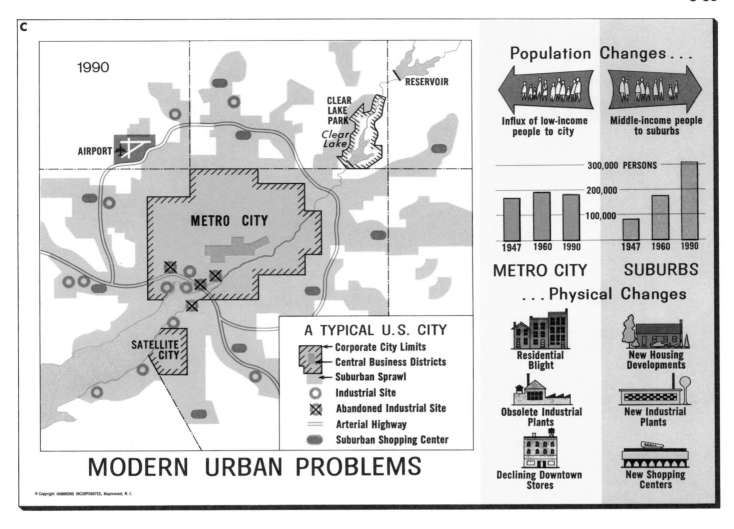

MODERN URBAN PROBLEMS

C — A TYPICAL U.S. CITY (1990)

Map labels: 1990, RESERVOIR, CLEAR LAKE PARK, Clear Lake, AIRPORT, METRO CITY, SATELLITE CITY

A TYPICAL U.S. CITY
- Corporate City Limits
- Central Business Districts
- Suburban Sprawl
- Industrial Site
- Abandoned Industrial Site
- Arterial Highway
- Suburban Shopping Center

Population Changes...
- Influx of low-income people to city
- Middle-income people to suburbs

300,000 PERSONS
200,000
100,000

METRO CITY: 1947, 1960, 1990
SUBURBS: 1947, 1960, 1990

...Physical Changes

METRO CITY:
- Residential Blight
- Obsolete Industrial Plants
- Declining Downtown Stores

SUBURBS:
- New Housing Developments
- New Industrial Plants
- New Shopping Centers

© Copyright HAMMOND INCORPORATED, Maplewood, N. J.

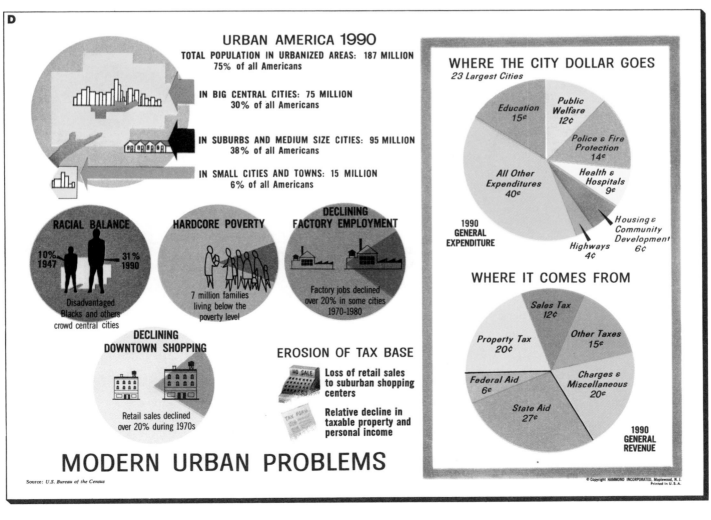

MODERN URBAN PROBLEMS

D

URBAN AMERICA 1990

TOTAL POPULATION IN URBANIZED AREAS: 187 MILLION
75% of all Americans

IN BIG CENTRAL CITIES: 75 MILLION
30% of all Americans

IN SUBURBS AND MEDIUM SIZE CITIES: 95 MILLION
38% of all Americans

IN SMALL CITIES AND TOWNS: 15 MILLION
6% of all Americans

RACIAL BALANCE
10% 1947 31% 1990
Disadvantaged Blacks and others crowd central cities

HARDCORE POVERTY
7 million families living below the poverty level

DECLINING FACTORY EMPLOYMENT
Factory jobs declined over 20% in some cities 1970-1980

DECLINING DOWNTOWN SHOPPING
Retail sales declined over 20% during 1970s

EROSION OF TAX BASE
NO SALE — Loss of retail sales to suburban shopping centers
TAX FORM — Relative decline in taxable property and personal income

WHERE THE CITY DOLLAR GOES
23 Largest Cities

- Education 15¢
- Public Welfare 12¢
- Police & Fire Protection 14¢
- Health & Hospitals 9¢
- Housing & Community Development 6¢
- Highways 4¢
- All Other Expenditures 40¢

1990 GENERAL EXPENDITURE

WHERE IT COMES FROM

- Sales Tax 12¢
- Other Taxes 15¢
- Property Tax 20¢
- Charges & Miscellaneous 20¢
- Federal Aid 6¢
- State Aid 27¢

1990 GENERAL REVENUE

Source: U.S. Bureau of the Census

© Copyright HAMMOND INCORPORATED, Maplewood, N. J.
Printed in U.S.A.

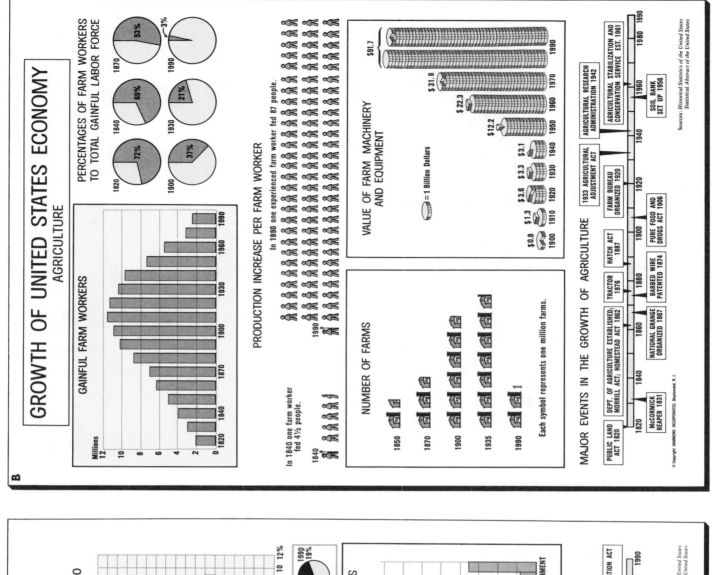

GROWTH OF UNITED STATES ECONOMY
POPULATION AND LABOR FORCE

POPULATION GROWTH 1820-1990

U.S. Percentage of World Total 1990 — 4.7%

POPULATION PYRAMID 1990

UNION MEMBERSHIP AS PERCENT OF TOTAL LABOR FORCE

1910 6% | 1930 7% | 1940 16% | 1950 22% | 1960 24% | 1970 23% | 1990 19%

SHIFTS IN RESIDENCY

1860 RURAL
1900 RURAL
1940 RURAL
1990 URBAN

EACH SYMBOL REPRESENTS 10% OF THE TOTAL POPULATION FOR EACH GIVEN YEAR.

SHIFTS IN MAJOR OCCUPATIONS 1920-1940-1990

MILLIONS OF WORKERS — FARMING, MANUFACTURING, TRADE & SERVICES, GOVERNMENT

MAJOR EVENTS IN THE LABOR MOVEMENT

WORKINGMEN'S PARTY 1828 | NATIONAL TRADES' UNION FOUNDED 1834 | NATIONAL LABOR UNION ORGANIZED 1866 | KNIGHTS OF LABOR FOUNDED 1869 | BUR. OF LABOR CREATED 1884 | AFL FOUNDED 1886 | DEPT OF LABOR ORGANIZED 1913 | 1932 NORRIS-LA GUARDIA ACT | WAGNER ACT 1935 | WAGES AND HOURS ACT, CIO FORMED 1938 | TAFT-HARTLEY ACT 1947 | AFL-CIO MERGER 1955 | LANDRUM-GRIFFIN ACT 1959 | RAILROAD ARBITRATION ACT 1963

Sources: Historical Statistics of the United States
Statistical Abstract of the United States

© Copyright HAMMOND INCORPORATED, Maplewood, N. J.
Printed in U. S. A.

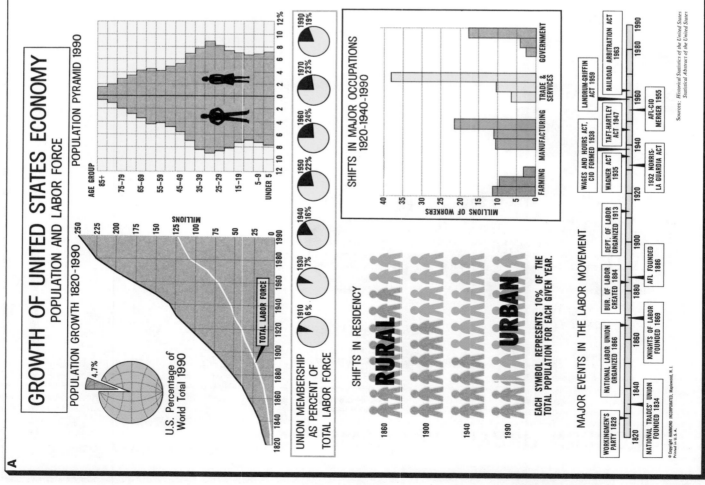

GROWTH OF UNITED STATES ECONOMY
AGRICULTURE

PERCENTAGES OF FARM WORKERS TO TOTAL GAINFUL LABOR FORCE

1820 72% | 1840 69% | 1870 53% | 1900 37% | 1930 21% | 1990 3%

GAINFUL FARM WORKERS

Millions — 1820 1840 1870 1900 1930 1960 1990

PRODUCTION INCREASE PER FARM WORKER

In 1840 one farm worker fed 4½ people.
In 1990 one experienced farm worker fed 87 people.

NUMBER OF FARMS

1850 | 1870 | 1900 | 1935 | 1990

Each symbol represents one million farms.

VALUE OF FARM MACHINERY AND EQUIPMENT

= 1 Billion Dollars

$0.8 1900 | $1.3 1910 | $3.6 1920 | $3.3 1930 | $3.1 1940 | $12.2 1950 | $22.3 1960 | $31.8 1970 | $91.7 1990

MAJOR EVENTS IN THE GROWTH OF AGRICULTURE

PUBLIC LAND ACT 1820 | McCORMICK REAPER 1831 | DEPT. OF AGRICULTURE ESTABLISHED; MORRILL ACT; HOMESTEAD ACT 1862 | NATIONAL GRANGE ORGANIZED 1867 | BARBED WIRE PATENTED 1874 | TRACTOR 1876 | HATCH ACT 1887 | PURE FOOD AND DRUGS ACT 1906 | FARM BUREAU ORGANIZED 1920 | 1933 AGRICULTURAL ADJUSTMENT ACT | AGRICULTURAL RESEARCH ADMINISTRATION 1942 | AGRICULTURAL STABILIZATION AND CONSERVATION SERVICE EST. 1961 | SOIL BANK SET UP 1956

Sources: Historical Statistics of the United States
Statistical Abstract of the United States

© Copyright HAMMOND INCORPORATED, Maplewood, N. J.

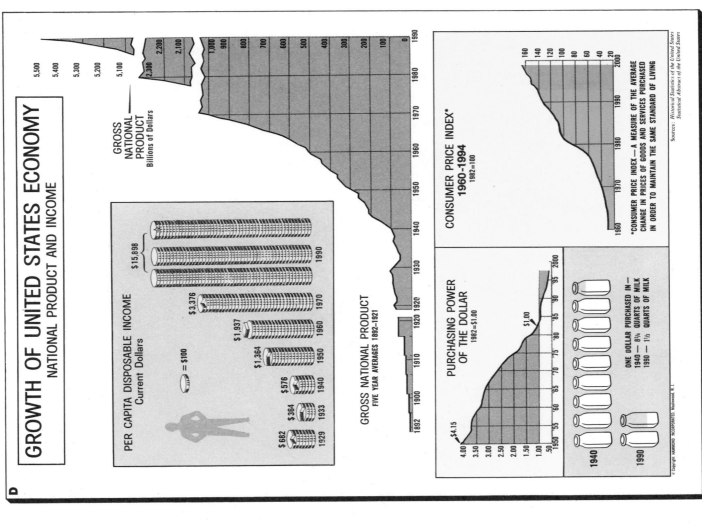

GROWTH OF UNITED STATES ECONOMY
NATIONAL PRODUCT AND INCOME

PER CAPITA DISPOSABLE INCOME
Current Dollars

= $100

$682	$364	$576	$1,364	$1,937	$3,376	$15,898
1929	1933	1940	1950	1960	1970	1990

GROSS NATIONAL PRODUCT
FIVE YEAR AVERAGES 1892-1921

GROSS NATIONAL PRODUCT
Billions of Dollars

CONSUMER PRICE INDEX*
1960-1994
1982=100

*CONSUMER PRICE INDEX — A MEASURE OF THE AVERAGE CHANGE IN PRICES OF GOODS AND SERVICES PURCHASED IN ORDER TO MAINTAIN THE SAME STANDARD OF LIVING

PURCHASING POWER OF THE DOLLAR
1982=$1.00

$4.15

$1.00

ONE DOLLAR PURCHASED IN —
1940 — 8¾ QUARTS OF MILK
1990 — 1⅓ QUARTS OF MILK

1940

1990

© Copyright HAMMOND INCORPORATED, Maplewood, N.J.

Sources: *Historical Statistics of the United States*
Statistical Abstract of the United States

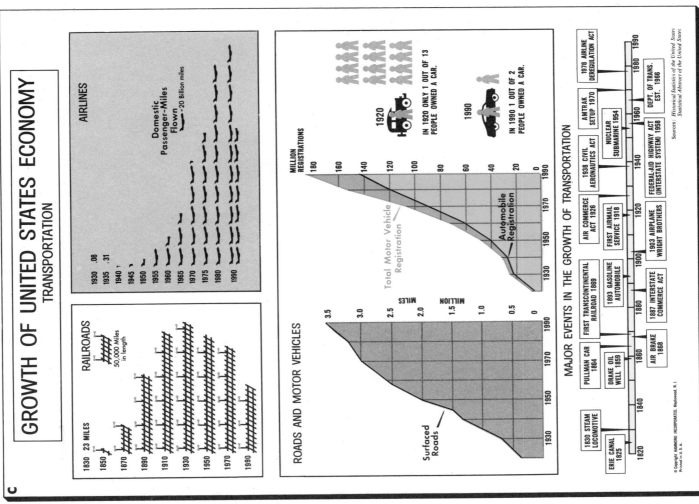

GROWTH OF UNITED STATES ECONOMY
TRANSPORTATION

RAILROADS
50,000 Miles in length

1830	23 MILES
1850	
1870	
1890	
1910	
1930	
1950	
1970	
1990	

AIRLINES
Domestic Passenger-Miles Flown
20 Billion miles

1930	.08
1935	.31
1940	
1945	
1950	
1955	
1960	
1965	
1970	
1975	
1980	
1990	

ROADS AND MOTOR VEHICLES

MILES   MILLION

Surfaced Roads

Total Motor Vehicle Registration

Automobile Registration

MILLION REGISTRATIONS

1920 — IN 1920 ONLY 1 OUT OF 13 PEOPLE OWNED A CAR.

1990 — IN 1990 1 OUT OF 2 PEOPLE OWNED A CAR.

MAJOR EVENTS IN THE GROWTH OF TRANSPORTATION

ERIE CANAL 1825
1830 STEAM LOCOMOTIVE
AIR BRAKE 1868
DRAKE OIL WELL 1859
PULLMAN CAR 1864
1887 INTERSTATE COMMERCE ACT
FIRST TRANSCONTINENTAL RAILROAD 1869
1893 GASOLINE AUTOMOBILE
1903 AIRPLANE WRIGHT BROTHERS
FIRST AIRMAIL SERVICE 1918
AIR COMMERCE ACT 1926
1938 CIVIL AERONAUTICS ACT
FEDERAL-AID HIGHWAY ACT (INTERSTATE SYSTEM) 1958
NUCLEAR SUBMARINE 1954
AMTRAK SETUP 1970
DEPT. OF TRANS. EST. 1966
1978 AIRLINE DEREGULATION ACT

Sources: *Historical Statistics of the United States*
Statistical Abstract of the United States

© Copyright HAMMOND INCORPORATED, Maplewood, N.J.
Printed in U.S.A.

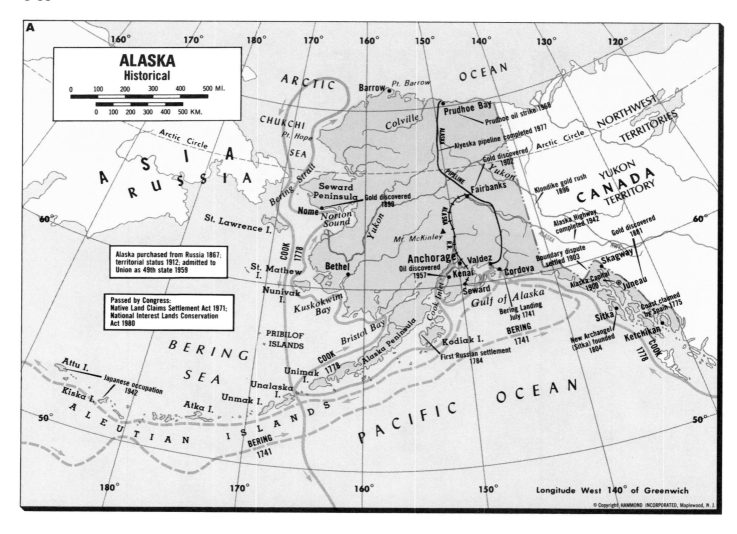

A

ALASKA
Historical

0 100 200 300 400 500 MI.

0 100 200 300 400 500 KM.

Alaska purchased from Russia 1867;
territorial status 1912; admitted to
Union as 49th state 1959

Passed by Congress:
Native Land Claims Settlement Act 1971;
National Interest Lands Conservation
Act 1980

ARCTIC OCEAN

Barrow · Pt. Barrow

Prudhoe Bay
Prudhoe oil strike 1968

Colville

Alyeska pipeline completed 1977

Arctic Circle

Gold discovered
1902

Arctic Circle

NORTHWEST
TERRITORIES

CHUKCHI
SEA

Pt. Hope

Bering Strait

ASIA
RUSSIA

Yukon

Fairbanks

Klondike gold rush
1896

YUKON
CANADA
TERRITORY

Seward
Peninsula
Gold discovered
1898

Alaska Highway
completed 1942

Gold discovered
1881

St. Lawrence I.

Nome · Norton
Sound

60°

Mt. McKinley ▲

Anchorage
Oil discovered
1957

Boundary dispute
settled 1903

60°

St. Mathew
I.

Bethel

COOK
1778

Valdez

Kenai

Cordova

Seward

Alaska Capital
1900

Skagway

Juneau

Nunivak
I.

Kuskokwim
Bay

Gulf of Alaska
Bering Landing
July 1741

Sitka

New Archangel
(Sitka) founded
1804

Coast claimed
by Spain 1775

PRIBILOF
· ISLANDS

Bristol Bay

COOK 1778

Alaska Peninsula

Kodiak I.

First Russian settlement
1784

BERING
1741

Ketchikan

COOK
1778

BERING
SEA

Attu I.
Japanese occupation
1942

Unimak
I.

Unalaska
I.

Unimak I.

1778

COOK

Kiska I.

Atka I.

ALEUTIAN ISLANDS

PACIFIC OCEAN

50°

BERING
1741

50°

180°

170°

160°

150°

Longitude West 140° of Greenwich

© Copyright HAMMOND INCORPORATED, Maplewood, N.J.

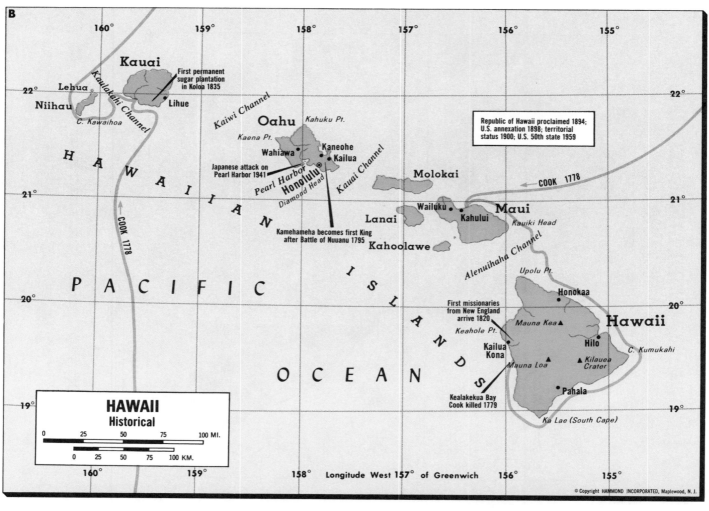

B

Kauai
First permanent
sugar plantation
in Koloa 1835

Lehua

Niihau

C. Kawaihoa

Kaulakahi Channel

Lihue

Kaiwi Channel

Oahu
Kahuku Pt.

Kaena Pt.

Wahiawa

Kaneohe
Kailua

Japanese attack on
Pearl Harbor 1941

Pearl Harbor
Honolulu
Diamond Head

Kauai Channel

Molokai

COOK 1778

Republic of Hawaii proclaimed 1894;
U.S. annexation 1898; territorial
status 1900; U.S. 50th state 1959

Wailuku

Maui

Kahului

Kauiki Head

HAWAIIAN

Lanai

Kamehameha becomes first King
after Battle of Nuuanu 1795

Kahoolawe

Alenuihaha Channel

Upolu Pt.

Honokaa

COOK 1778

First missionaries
from New England
arrive 1820

Mauna Kea ▲

Keahole Pt.

Hawaii

Hilo

C. Kumukahi

Kailua
Kona

Mauna Loa ▲

▲ Kilauea
Crater

ISLANDS

Kealakekua Bay
Cook killed 1779

Pahala

HAWAII
Historical

0 25 50 75 100 MI.

0 25 50 75 100 KM.

PACIFIC OCEAN

Ka Lae (South Cape)

160°

159°

158°

Longitude West 157° of Greenwich

156°

155°

© Copyright HAMMOND INCORPORATED, Maplewood, N.J.

THE FIFTY STATES

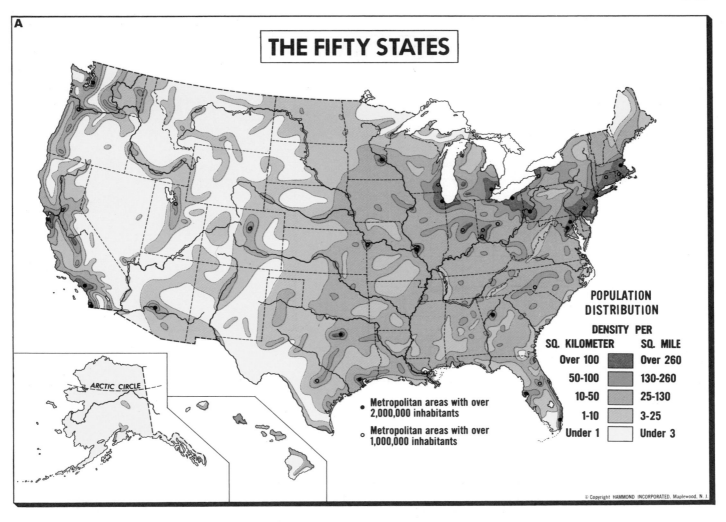

POPULATION DISTRIBUTION

DENSITY PER

SQ. KILOMETER	SQ. MILE
Over 100	Over 260
50-100	130-260
10-50	25-130
1-10	3-25
Under 1	Under 3

● Metropolitan areas with over 2,000,000 inhabitants

○ Metropolitan areas with over 1,000,000 inhabitants

ARCTIC CIRCLE

© Copyright HAMMOND INCORPORATED, Maplewood, N.J.

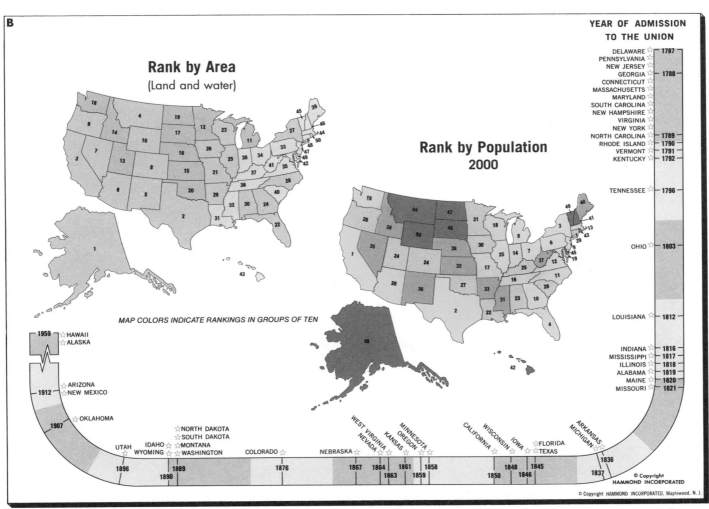

Rank by Area
(Land and water)

Rank by Population
2000

MAP COLORS INDICATE RANKINGS IN GROUPS OF TEN

YEAR OF ADMISSION TO THE UNION

State	Year
DELAWARE ☆	1787
PENNSYLVANIA ☆	
NEW JERSEY ☆	
GEORGIA ☆	1788
CONNECTICUT ☆	
MASSACHUSETTS ☆	
MARYLAND ☆	
SOUTH CAROLINA ☆	
NEW HAMPSHIRE ☆	
VIRGINIA ☆	
NEW YORK ☆	
NORTH CAROLINA ☆	1789
RHODE ISLAND ☆	1790
VERMONT ☆	1791
KENTUCKY ☆	1792
TENNESSEE ☆	1796
OHIO ☆	1803
LOUISIANA ☆	1812
INDIANA ☆	1816
MISSISSIPPI ☆	1817
ILLINOIS ☆	1818
ALABAMA ☆	1819
MAINE ☆	1820
MISSOURI ☆	1821

1959 ☆ HAWAII
☆ ALASKA

1912 ☆ ARIZONA
☆ NEW MEXICO

1907 ☆ OKLAHOMA

☆ NORTH DAKOTA
☆ SOUTH DAKOTA
UTAH ☆ ☆ MONTANA
IDAHO ☆
WYOMING ☆ ☆ WASHINGTON

COLORADO ☆

WEST VIRGINIA ☆
NEVADA ☆
KANSAS ☆
NEBRASKA ☆
OREGON ☆
MINNESOTA ☆

CALIFORNIA ☆
WISCONSIN ☆
IOWA ☆
☆ FLORIDA
☆ TEXAS

ARKANSAS ☆
MICHIGAN ☆

| 1896 | 1889 | 1876 | 1867 | 1864 | 1861 | 1858 | 1848 | 1845 | 1836 |
| | 1890 | | | 1863 | | 1859 | 1850 | 1846 | 1837 |

© Copyright HAMMOND INCORPORATED
© Copyright HAMMOND INCORPORATED, Maplewood, N.J.

POPULATION CHARACTERISTICS

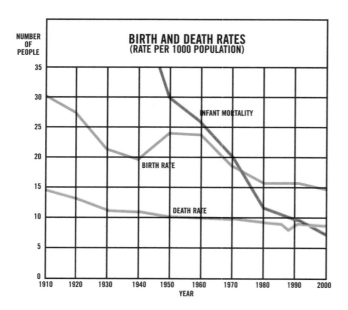

BIRTH AND DEATH RATES
(RATE PER 1000 POPULATION)

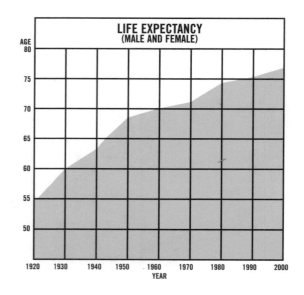

LIFE EXPECTANCY
(MALE AND FEMALE)

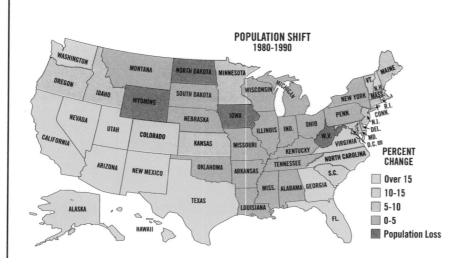

POPULATION SHIFT
1980-1990

PERCENT CHANGE
- Over 15
- 10-15
- 5-10
- 0-5
- Population Loss

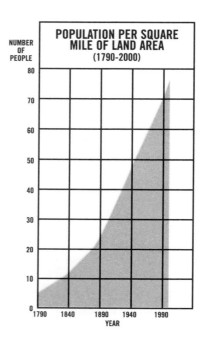

POPULATION PER SQUARE MILE OF LAND AREA
(1790-2000)

POPULATION SHIFT
1990-2000

PERCENT CHANGE
- Over 15
- 10-15
- 5-10
- 0-5
- Population Loss

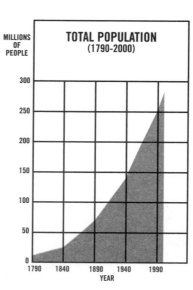

TOTAL POPULATION
(1790-2000)

Source: *Statistical Abstract of the US*

© Copyright HAMMOND World Atlas Corporation

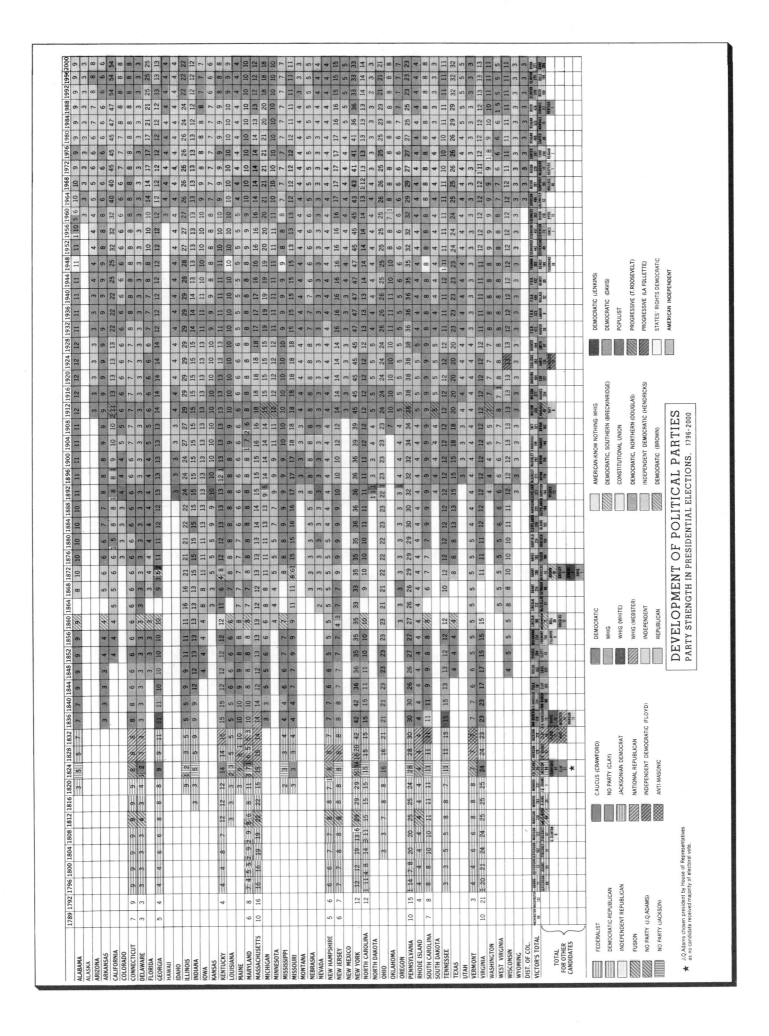

DEVELOPMENT OF POLITICAL PARTIES
PARTY STRENGTH IN PRESIDENTIAL ELECTIONS, 1796-2000

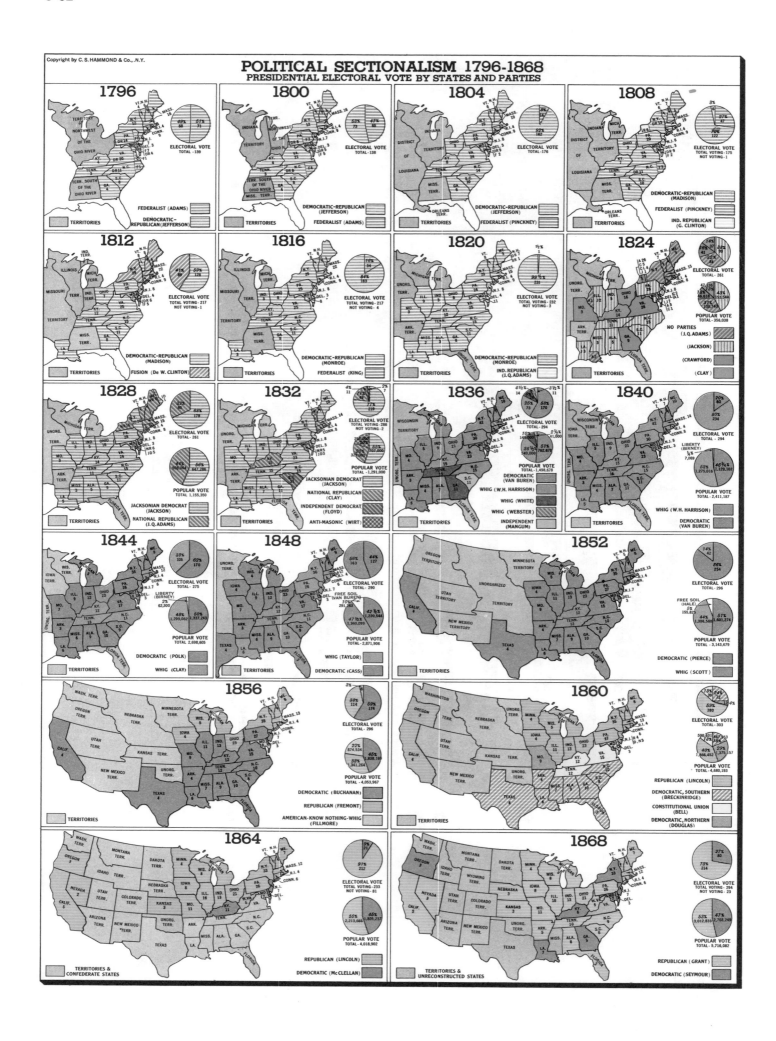

POLITICAL SECTIONALISM 1796-1868
PRESIDENTIAL ELECTORAL VOTE BY STATES AND PARTIES

Copyright by C. S. HAMMOND & Co., N.Y.

Copyright by C.S. HAMMOND & Co., N.Y.

POLITICAL SECTIONALISM 1872-1916
PRESIDENTIAL ELECTORAL VOTE BY STATES AND PARTIES

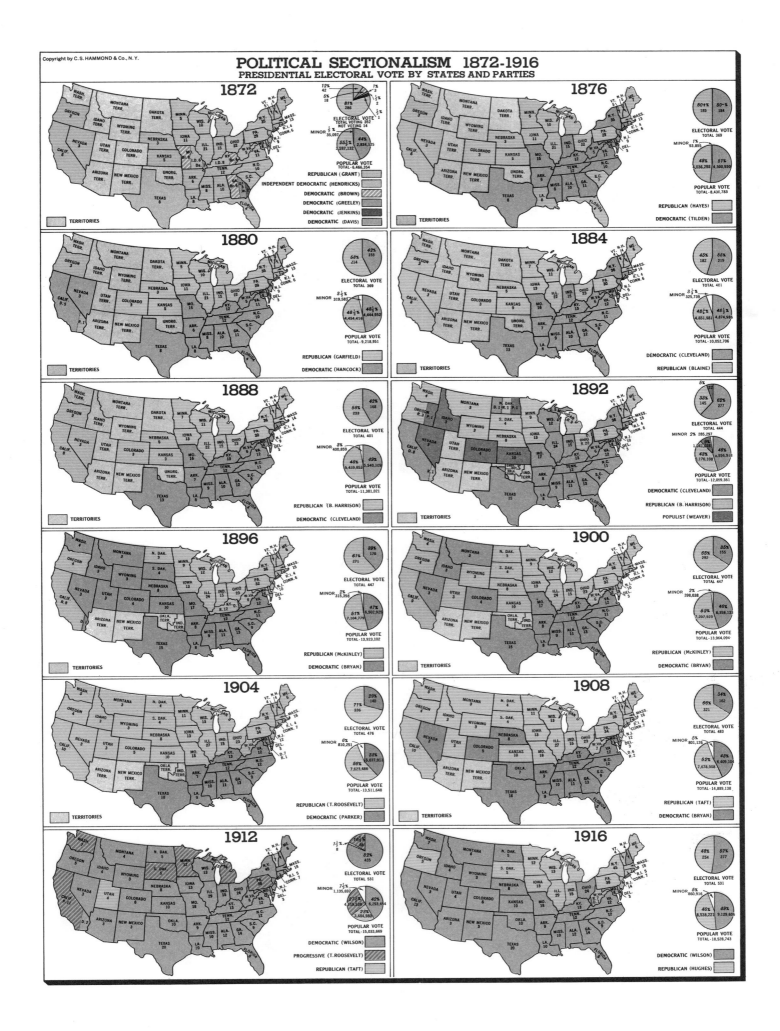

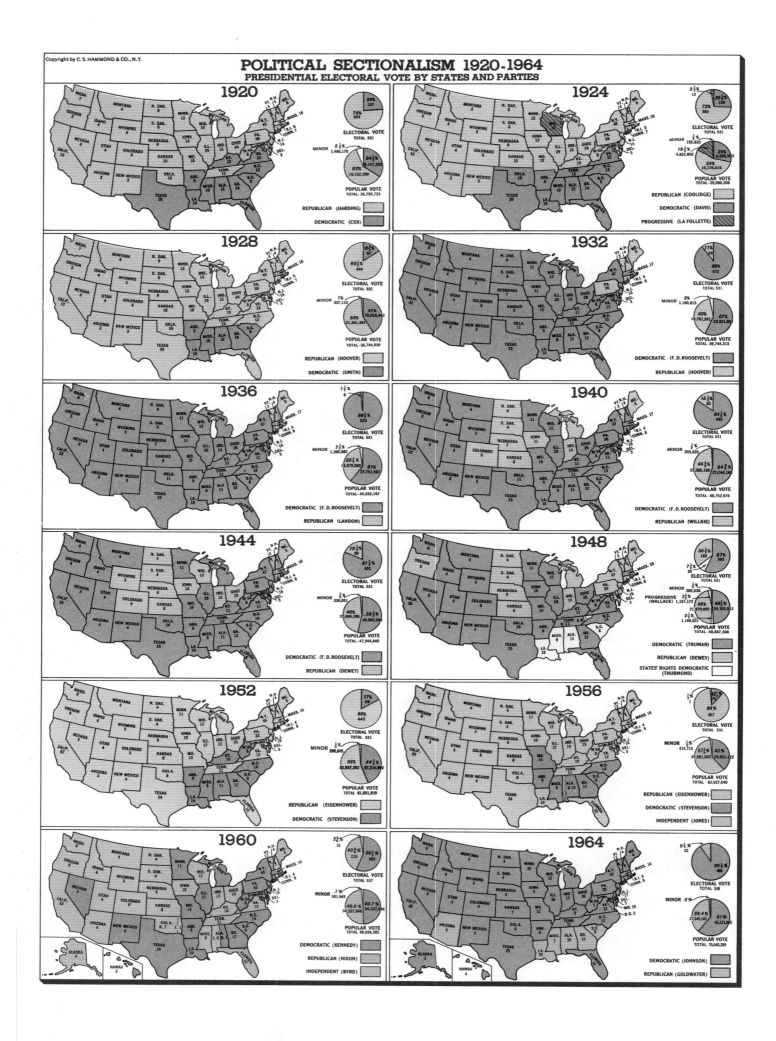

Copyright by C. S. HAMMOND & CO., N.Y.

POLITICAL SECTIONALISM 1920-1964
PRESIDENTIAL ELECTORAL VOTE BY STATES AND PARTIES

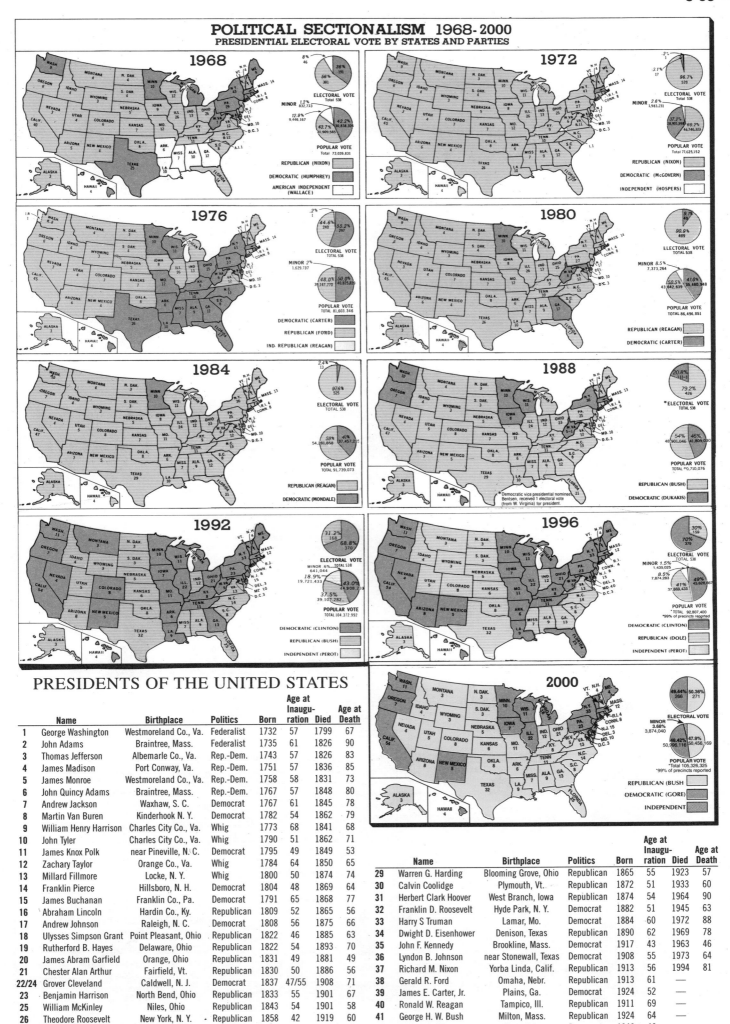

POLITICAL SECTIONALISM 1968-2000
PRESIDENTIAL ELECTORAL VOTE BY STATES AND PARTIES

1968

ELECTORAL VOTE Total 538

MINOR 1.2% 832,733

POPULAR VOTE Total 73,026,831

REPUBLICAN (NIXON)
DEMOCRATIC (HUMPHREY)
AMERICAN INDEPENDENT (WALLACE)

1972

ELECTORAL VOTE Total 538

MINOR 2.6% 1,983,231

POPULAR VOTE Total 77,625,152

REPUBLICAN (NIXON)
DEMOCRATIC (McGOVERN)
INDEPENDENT (HOSPERS)

1976

ELECTORAL VOTE TOTAL 538

MINOR 2% 1,629,737

POPULAR VOTE TOTAL 81,603,346

DEMOCRATIC (CARTER)
REPUBLICAN (FORD)
IND. REPUBLICAN (REAGAN)

1980

ELECTORAL VOTE TOTAL 538

MINOR 8.5% 7,373,264

POPULAR VOTE TOTAL 86,496,851

REPUBLICAN (REAGAN)
DEMOCRATIC (CARTER)

1984

ELECTORAL VOTE TOTAL 538

POPULAR VOTE TOTAL 91,739,073

REPUBLICAN (REAGAN)
DEMOCRATIC (MONDALE)

1988

*ELECTORAL VOTE TOTAL 538

POPULAR VOTE TOTAL 90,710,076

*Democratic vice presidential nominee, Bentsen, received 1 electoral vote (from W. Virginia) for president.

REPUBLICAN (BUSH)
DEMOCRATIC (DUKAKIS)

1992

ELECTORAL VOTE TOTAL 538

MINOR 6% 641,044

POPULAR VOTE TOTAL 104,372,992

DEMOCRATIC (CLINTON)
REPUBLICAN (BUSH)
INDEPENDENT (PEROT)

1996

ELECTORAL VOTE TOTAL 538

MINOR 1.5% 1,435,025

POPULAR VOTE *TOTAL 92,807,400
*99% of precincts reported

DEMOCRATIC (CLINTON)
REPUBLICAN (DOLE)
INDEPENDENT (PEROT)

2000

ELECTORAL VOTE

MINOR 3.68% 3,874,040

POPULAR VOTE *Total 105,326,325
*99% of precincts reported

REPUBLICAN (BUSH)
DEMOCRATIC (GORE)
INDEPENDENT

PRESIDENTS OF THE UNITED STATES

	Name	Birthplace	Politics	Born	Age at Inauguration	Died	Age at Death
1	George Washington	Westmoreland Co., Va.	Federalist	1732	57	1799	67
2	John Adams	Braintree, Mass.	Federalist	1735	61	1826	90
3	Thomas Jefferson	Albemarle Co., Va.	Rep.-Dem.	1743	57	1826	83
4	James Madison	Port Conway, Va.	Rep.-Dem.	1751	57	1836	85
5	James Monroe	Westmoreland Co., Va.	Rep.-Dem.	1758	58	1831	73
6	John Quincy Adams	Braintree, Mass.	Rep.-Dem.	1767	57	1848	80
7	Andrew Jackson	Waxhaw, S. C.	Democrat	1767	61	1845	78
8	Martin Van Buren	Kinderhook N. Y.	Democrat	1782	54	1862	79
9	William Henry Harrison	Charles City Co., Va.	Whig	1773	68	1841	68
10	John Tyler	Charles City Co., Va.	Whig	1790	51	1862	71
11	James Knox Polk	near Pineville, N. C.	Democrat	1795	49	1849	53
12	Zachary Taylor	Orange Co., Va.	Whig	1784	64	1850	65
13	Millard Fillmore	Locke, N. Y.	Whig	1800	50	1874	74
14	Franklin Pierce	Hillsboro, N. H.	Democrat	1804	48	1869	64
15	James Buchanan	Franklin Co., Pa.	Democrat	1791	65	1868	77
16	Abraham Lincoln	Hardin Co., Ky.	Republican	1809	52	1865	56
17	Andrew Johnson	Raleigh, N. C.	Democrat	1808	56	1875	66
18	Ulysses Simpson Grant	Point Pleasant, Ohio	Republican	1822	46	1885	63
19	Rutherford B. Hayes	Delaware, Ohio	Republican	1822	54	1893	70
20	James Abram Garfield	Orange, Ohio	Republican	1831	49	1881	49
21	Chester Alan Arthur	Fairfield, Vt.	Republican	1830	50	1886	56
22/24	Grover Cleveland	Caldwell, N. J.	Democrat	1837	47/55	1908	71
23	Benjamin Harrison	North Bend, Ohio	Republican	1833	55	1901	67
25	William McKinley	Niles, Ohio	Republican	1843	54	1901	58
26	Theodore Roosevelt	New York, N. Y.	Republican	1858	42	1919	60
27	William Howard Taft	Cincinnati, Ohio	Republican	1857	51	1930	72
28	Woodrow Wilson	Staunton, Va.	Democrat	1856	56	1924	67
29	Warren G. Harding	Blooming Grove, Ohio	Republican	1865	55	1923	57
30	Calvin Coolidge	Plymouth, Vt.	Republican	1872	51	1933	60
31	Herbert Clark Hoover	West Branch, Iowa	Republican	1874	54	1964	90
32	Franklin D. Roosevelt	Hyde Park, N. Y.	Democrat	1882	51	1945	63
33	Harry S Truman	Lamar, Mo.	Democrat	1884	60	1972	88
34	Dwight D. Eisenhower	Denison, Texas	Republican	1890	62	1969	78
35	John F. Kennedy	Brookline, Mass.	Democrat	1917	43	1963	46
36	Lyndon B. Johnson	near Stonewall, Texas	Democrat	1908	55	1973	64
37	Richard M. Nixon	Yorba Linda, Calif.	Republican	1913	56	1994	81
38	Gerald R. Ford	Omaha, Nebr.	Republican	1913	61	—	
39	James E. Carter, Jr.	Plains, Ga.	Democrat	1924	52	—	
40	Ronald W. Reagan	Tampico, Ill.	Republican	1911	69	—	
41	George H. W. Bush	Milton, Mass.	Republican	1924	64	—	
42	William J. Clinton	Hope, Ark.	Democrat	1946	46	—	
43	George W. Bush	New Haven, Conn.	Republican	1946	54	—	

Flags of American History

FLAGS OF DISCOVERY AND SETTLEMENT

FLAG OF LEIF ERICKSON—1000
RAVEN OF THE VIKINGS, FIRST FLAG CARRIED TO AMERICA'S SHORES.

EXPEDITIONARY FLAG OF COLUMBUS 1492

FLAG OF COLUMBUS 1492–1498
STANDARD OF FERDINAND AND ISABELLA. RAISED AT SAN SALVADOR 1492, MAINLAND, 1498.

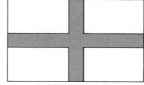

FLAG OF JOHN CABOT—1497
CROSS OF ST. GEORGE. FIRST FLAG RAISED ON MAINLAND. RALEIGH'S FLAG 1585.

FLAG OF CHAMPLAIN—1603
BORNE BY CARTIER, JOLIET, MARQUETTE, LA SALLE AND OTHER INTREPID FRENCH VOYAGEURS.

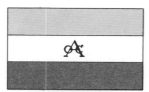

FLAG OF HUDSON—1607
FIRST FLAG RAISED AT NEW YORK, VERRAZANO DISCOVERED THE RIVER EIGHTY FOUR YEARS EARLIER.

FLAG OF THE MAYFLOWER—1620
FLAG BORNE ON THE MAIN MAST OF THE MAYFLOWER BY THE PILGRIM FATHERS.

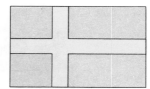

FLAG OF SWEDEN—1638
ENSIGN OF NEW SWEDEN RAISED ON THE DELAWARE RIVER.

FLAGS OF COLONIAL DAYS

STUART STANDARD 1603–1649, 1660–1689

CROMWELL'S STANDARD 1653–1660

ROYAL STANDARD 1689–1702

ROYAL STANDARD 1707–1714

ROYAL STANDARD 1714–1801

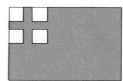

ENGLISH RED ENSIGN
THE FAMOUS METEOR FLAG OF OLD ENGLAND AND ENSIGN OF COLONIES 17th CENTURY.

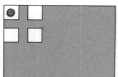

ENDICOTT FLAG—1634
THE SALEM ENSIGN SHOWING RELIGIOUS OPPOSITION TO CROSS IN CANTON.

THREE COUNTY TROUP—1659
FLAG OF THE THREE MASSACHUSETTS COUNTIES AND EMBLEM OF KING PHILIP'S WAR, 1675–1676.

ESCUTCHEONED JACK—1701
FLAG DESIGNED FOR MERCHANT SHIPS OF HIS MAJESTY'S PLANTATIONS.

NEW ENGLAND FLAG—1737
THIS ENSIGN SHOWS THE EARLY TENDENCY OF THE COLONIES TO FIND INDIVIDUAL FLAGS.

FLAGS OF THE REVOLUTION

TAUNTON FLAG—1774
ONE OF THE EARLIEST EMBLEMS OF THE REVOLUTION.

BEDFORD FLAG—1775
CARRIED BY REVERE AND DAWES IN AROUSING THE MINUTE MEN.

CULPEPER FLAG—1775
ONE OF THE EARLY RATTLESNAKE FLAGS CARRIED BY THE MINUTE MEN.

PHILADELPHIA LIGHT HORSE
WASHINGTON'S ESCORT TO COMMAND OF THE CONTINENTAL ARMY, 1775.

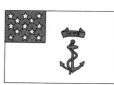

RHODE ISLAND FLAG—1776
CARRIED AT BRANDYWINE, TRENTON AND YORKTOWN.

FORT MOULTRIE FLAG—1776
NAILED TO STAFF BY SERGEANT JASPER WHEN SHOT AWAY.

LIBERTY TREE FLAG—1776
THE PINE TREE COMES FROM COINS OF THE COLONY OF MASSACHUSETTS, 1652.

BENNINGTON FLAG—1777
FLAG OF VICTORY OF THE GREEN MOUNTAIN BOYS.

BENJAMIN FRANKLIN FLAG
ALSO CALLED "SERAPIS" FLAG. GENERALLY ACCEPTED AS ORIGINATED BY BENJAMIN FRANKLIN AT COURT OF LOUIS XVI.

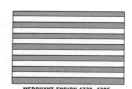

MERCHANT ENSIGN 1776–1795
AN EMBLEM IN GENERAL USE, ALSO PRIVATEER'S FLAG.

FLAGS OF THE OLD NAVY

GADSDEN FLAG—1775
COMMODORE ESEK HOPKINS' ENSIGN USED IN HIS FIRST FLEET COMMAND.

WASHINGTON'S NAVY ENSIGN—1775
THE FLAG OF THE SIX CRUISERS THAT FORMED THE FIRST AMERICAN NAVAL FLEET.

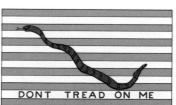

FIRST NAVY JACK—1775
HOSTED AT THE MAIN MAST BY COMMANDER-IN-CHIEF ESEK HOPKINS, DECEMBER 3, 1775.

© Copyright 1989 by HAMMOND INCORPORATED, Maplewood, N.J.

FLAGS OF THE YOUNG REPUBLIC

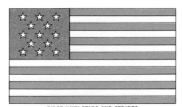

FIRST NAVY STARS AND STRIPES
IN ABSENCE OF SPECIFIC ARRANGEMENT OF STARS BY CONGRESS JUNE 14, 1777 IT WAS CUSTOMARY FOR NAVY TO PLACE THE STARS IN FORM OF CROSSES OF ST. GEORGE AND ST. ANDREW.

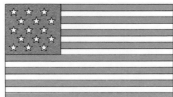

"STAR SPANGLED BANNER" —1814
THE EMBLEM OF INSPIRATION OF OUR NATIONAL ANTHEM, 1814. FLAG OF VICTORY OVER BARBARY PIRATES 1803 TO 1805.

FREMONT THE PATHFINDER'S FLAG—40'S
EMBLEM THAT BLAZED THE TRAIL FOR THE COVERED WAGON IN THE ROARING 40'S. THE EARLY ENSIGN OF THE PLAINS.

FAMOUS BATTLE FLAGS

BUNKER HILL FLAG—1775
HISTORIC EMBLEM THAT PROVED THE STRENGTH OF THE SPIRIT OF AMERICAN LIBERTY. CARRIED AT LEXINGTON AND CONCORD.

CAMBRIDGE FLAG, FIRST NAVY ENSIGN 1775–1776
HOISTED BY JOHN PAUL JONES, DECEMBER 3, 1775 AND BY GENERAL WASHINGTON, JANUARY 2, 1776.

CONTINENTAL FLAG
CARRIED IN 1775–1777, SHOWING PINE TREE, SYMBOL OF MASSACHUSETTS BAY COLONY, IN PLACE OF THE CROSSES OF ST. GEORGE AND ST. ANDREW.

FLAGS OF THE CONFEDERACY

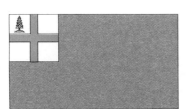

FIRST CONFEDERATE FLAG
FAMOUS "STARS AND BARS" USED FROM MARCH 1861 TO MAY 1863.

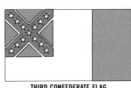

SECOND CONFEDERATE FLAG
NATIONAL EMBLEM FROM MAY 1, 1863 TO MARCH 4, 1865.

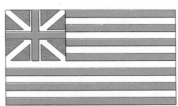

THIRD CONFEDERATE FLAG
NATIONAL EMBLEM ADOPTED MARCH 8, 1865.

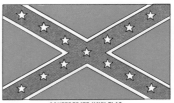

CONFEDERATE NAVY FLAG
USED FROM MAY 1, 1863 TO END OF WAR, 1865. THE BATTLE FLAG WAS SQUARE.

OTHER NOTEWORTHY FLAGS OF AMERICAN HISTORY

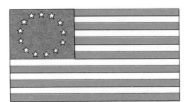

FIRST STARS AND STRIPES
UNITED EMBLEM OF INDEPENDENCE SAID TO HAVE ORIGINATED BY GEORGE WASHINGTON FOLLOWING ACT OF CONGRESS OF JUNE 14, 1777.

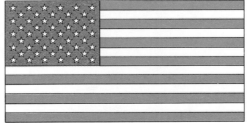

PRESENT DAY FLAG

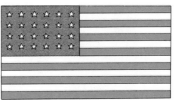

"OLD GLORY"
NAME GIVEN BY CAPTAIN WILLIAM DRIVER, COMMANDING THE BRIG "CHARLES DAGGETT" IN 1831.

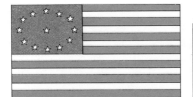

FLAG OF THE THIRD MARYLAND REGIMENT—1778
CARRIED AT THE BATTLE OF COWPENS JANUARY, 1778 AND USED AS COLORS OF AMERICAN LAND FORCES UNTIL MEXICAN WAR.

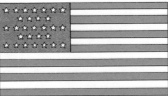

FLAG OF THE MEXICAN WAR—1845
NOT ACTUALLY USED AS REGIMENTAL COLORS BY TROOPS, BUT AS FLAG OF CONQUEST AND OCCUPATION.

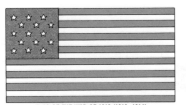

FLAG OF THE WAR OF 1812 (1812–1814)
SHOWING FIFTEEN STARS AND FIFTEEN BARS AS CHANGED UPON ADMISSION OF VERMONT.

NAPOLEON'S LOUISIANA FLAG
THIS FLAG WAS REPLACED BY "STARS AND STRIPES" FOLLOWING LOUISIANA PURCHASE DECEMBER 24, 1803.

U.S. NAVY JACK
USED BY NAVAL VESSELS AND MARITIME GOVERNORS.

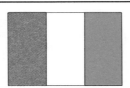

RUSSIAN AMERICAN CO'S. FLAG
EMBLEM RAISED 1799, REPLACED BY "STARS AND STRIPES" 1867.

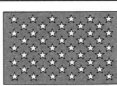

U.S. COAST GUARD FLAG
WITHOUT EMBLEM ON FLY THIS IS U.S. CUSTOMS FLAG.

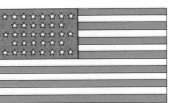

FLAG OF THE CIVIL WAR 1861–1865
THE "STARS AND STRIPES" WITH THIRTY SIX STARS IN THE UNION CARRIED BY THE NORTHERN ARMIES DURING LATER YEARS OF THE CIVIL WAR.

THE FLAG OF 1818
SHOWING RETURN TO THIRTEEN STRIPES AND ADDITIONAL STARS IN CANTON.

COMMODORE PERRY'S FLAG—1854
THE FLAG THAT OPENED JAPAN TO WESTERN CIVILIZATION.

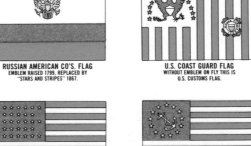

AMERICAN YACHT ENSIGN
AUTHORIZED BY ACT OF CONGRESS AUGUST 7, 1848.

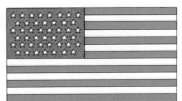

FLAG OF THE SPANISH-AMERICAN WAR—1898
THE EMBLEM OF LIBERTY THAT BROUGHT FREEDOM TO CUBA.

© Copyright 1989 by HAMMOND INCORPORATED, Maplewood, N.J.

UNITED STATES

LEGEND

Capitals of Countries	**Washington**
State / Provincial Capitals	Sacramento
International Boundaries	—·—·—
State / Provincial Boundaries	—·—·—
National Parks	▨ ♣
Mountain Peak	▲
Dam	●

Population of Cities & Towns

Over 2,000,000	▣
1,000,000 - 1,999,999	▢
500,000 - 999,999	◉
100,000 - 499,999	⊛
50,000 - 99,999	⊕
Under 50,000	·

SCALE 1:12,000,000
LAMBERT CONFORMAL CONIC PROJECTION

0 —————— 200 Mi.
0 —————— 200 Km.

© HAMMOND WORLD ATLAS CORPORATION

Flags of States, Territories and Possessions

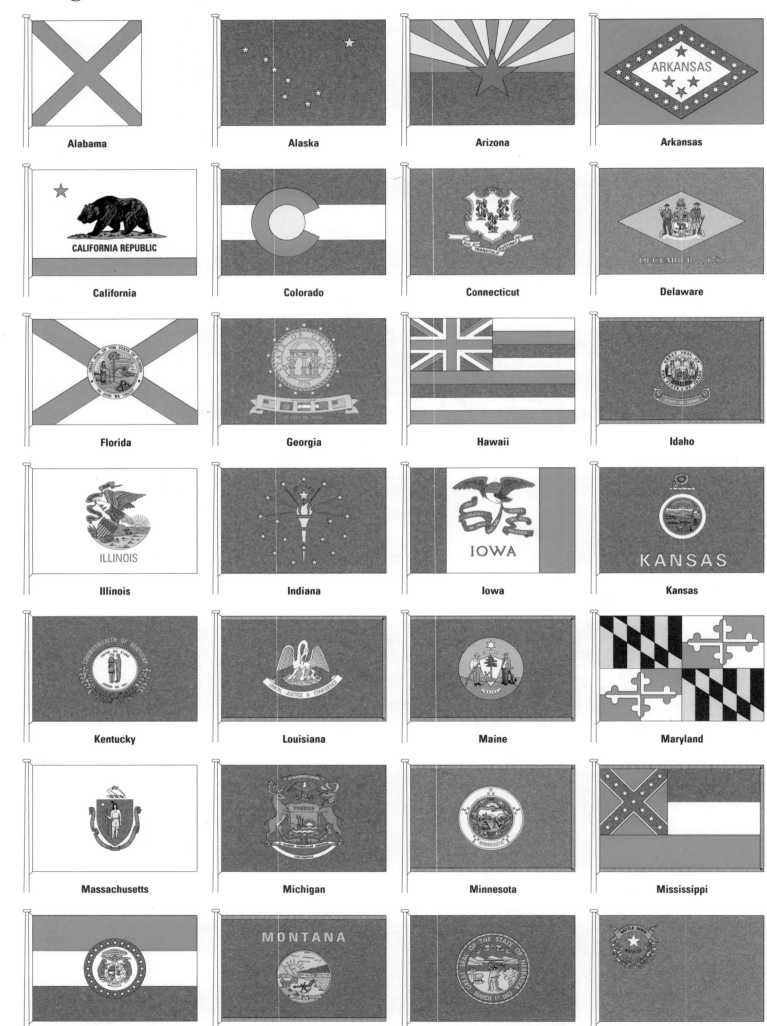

Alabama	**Alaska**	**Arizona**	**Arkansas**
California	**Colorado**	**Connecticut**	**Delaware**
Florida	**Georgia**	**Hawaii**	**Idaho**
Illinois	**Indiana**	**Iowa**	**Kansas**
Kentucky	**Louisiana**	**Maine**	**Maryland**
Massachusetts	**Michigan**	**Minnesota**	**Mississippi**
Missouri	**Montana**	**Nebraska**	**Nevada**